Kids' Cookbook

Kids' Cookbook

Bridget Jones

THE
APPLE
PRESS

A QUINTET BOOK

Published by The Apple Press
6 Blundell Street
London N7 9BH

ISBN 1-85076-207-4

This book was designed and produced by
Quintet Publishing Limited
6 Blundell Street
London N7 9BH

Creative Director: Peter Bridgewater
Designer and Illustrator: Sally McKay
Editor: Barbara Fuller
Photographer: Ian Howes

Typeset in Great Britain by
Central Southern Typesetters, Eastbourne
Manufactured in Hong Kong by
Regent Publishing Services Limited
Printed in Hong Kong
by Kwong Fat Offset Printing Company Limited

CONTENTS

BEFORE YOU START

Cooking is fun. To make sure you enjoy cooking and the food tastes good enough to eat, read through these notes first.

★ Always ask if you can cook.
★ Make sure you have an adult in the kitchen to help.
★ Put an apron on to keep your clothes clean. Having an apron on also keeps your clothes away from the food and the cooker.
★ Keep long sleeves rolled up out of the way.
★ Wash your hands really well in hot soapy water.
★ Read through the recipe first.
★ Find all the ingredients and put them out ready.
★ Set out all the utensils.
★ Keep a clean, damp dish cloth near to wipe up any mess.

Now you may begin!

SAFE AND CLEAN

Remember that what you are cooking is going to be eaten. The food must be kept clean all the time. If you have an accident while you are cooking, there will not be any food to eat. So always remember the S + C Rules.

★ Make sure you have an adult near when you are using the hob, grill or cooker.
★ Always use oven gloves when you are handling hot dishes.
★ Put a heatproof mat on the work surface before taking hot pans and dishes from the hob, grill or oven.
★ When you put pans on the hob make sure the handles are pointing to the side, not out in front where you may knock them.
★ Always watch food which is cooking under the grill.

★ As soon as you have finished cooking food turn off the heat.
★ Take extra care when using knives. Make sure the knife is the right size so that you can hold it properly.
★ Keep your fingers out of the way when cutting and chopping. Cut slowly to get it right.
★ Always wash your knife and scrub the board after cutting raw fish, meat or chicken and before cutting up any other ingredients.
★ Keep the work surface clean by wiping up as you are cooking.
★ If you spill anything wipe it up at once.
★ Don't forget to wash up and tidy the kitchen!

USING THE MICROWAVE

The microwave cooker is safe to use because it is not as hot as the hob or oven. You must remember to use it properly.

★ Never put baking tins, cooking foil or wire bag ties in the microwave.
★ Never switch the microwave on without any food in it.
★ Take care when setting the timer. Check you have the right cooking time.
★ Check that you are using the correct power setting.
★ Always cook food for a short time. Take it out and stir or turn the food before cooking again for a short time.
★ Remember that the food gets very hot. Use an oven glove to take dishes from the microwave.
★ When you think the food is cooked, check that it is cooked through. Stir wet foods before serving. If parts of the food are cold or not cooked, then put it back in the microwave and cook for another short time.

★ There are microwave notes for some of the recipes. The times are for a 650 watt cooker. Ask what power your microwave cooks at and check that it is the same. If it has a lower power, the cooking will take a little longer. If it has a higher power the food will cook more quickly.

WEIGHING AND MEASURING INGREDIENTS

All the recipes in this book give the quantities in metric and Imperial measures. You must follow one set of quantities for each recipe.

WEIGHING

You need a pair of kitchen scales to weigh food. Practise by weighing some vegetables. When you have tried weighing a few items you will see how your scales work.

MEASURING TEASPOONS AND TABLESPOONS

When a recipe tells you to add 1 teaspoon of something, or 2 tablespoons, you must use proper measuring spoons.

★ Measuring spoons come in small sets. They include ¼ teaspoon, ½ teaspoon, 1 teaspoon and 1 tablespoon. Each spoon will have the size written on it.
★ Use the right size spoon. Fill the spoon with the ingredient. Use a knife to level the top of the spoon when measuring dry ingredients.
★ Hold the spoon steady and level for a few seconds when measuring liquid to check that it is full.

MEASURING LIQUID

★ Pour the liquid into a measuring jug and put it on a level surface.
★ Look at the side of the jug to see if the liquid is up to the mark you want. If

not add more. If there is too much in the jug, pour a little out, put it back on the level and check again.

WHAT IS A . . .

KITCHEN KNIFE

For chopping up food you will need a sharp kitchen knife, also called a chef's knife. Make sure it is not too big to handle.

PALETTE KNIFE OR BLUNT KNIFE

This is a knife with a rounded end. It does not have a sharp edge. Some dinner knives are blunt so they may be used instead of a palette knife. A palette knife is used to lift biscuits off baking trays or to spread butter, icing or soft cheese.

CHOPPING BOARD

When you cut something always use a chopping board. Make sure that the board is safe and firm on the work surface. If the surface is slippery, put a piece of absorbent kitchen paper under the board. Plastic boards are more advisable than wooden ones because they are easier to clean. When you have finished cooking you must scrub the chopping board with a brush and kitchen cleaner.

GRATER

There are lots of different types. They have fine or coarse blades. Always take care when grating food – it is easy to grate the end of your fingers and it hurts!

LEMON SQUEEZER

Some recipes tell you to squeeze the juice from a lemon or orange. You have to cut the fruit in half, then hold one half on a lemon squeezer. Twist the fruit around, pressing it down on the squeezer to get all the juice out.

WHISK

This is used for whisking eggs and for whipping cream. A hand whisk is made up of wire loops and a handle. A rotary whisk has 2 metal whisks that are turned by you turning a handle. An electric whisk is very quick but you should never use one unless you have an adult with you.

SIEVE

This is used for sifting flour that may be lumpy. It is also used for making a purée, or paste, out of food. Stand the sieve firmly over a bowl before putting the food in it.

PASTRY BRUSH

This is a small brush made for kitchen use. A pastry brush is used for brushing pastry and other foods with egg, milk or water. After you have grated fruit rind, use a pastry brush to brush all the rind off the grater.

COLANDER

A bowl with holes in it. This is used to drain food. Cooked pasta is drained in a colander. Shredded cabbage or lettuce may be put in a colander to drain when it has been washed. Always put the colander in the sink or over a bowl.

BAKING TRAY

A flat metal tray used for baking biscuits and other foods in the oven. Sometimes a baking tray is covered with paper or cling film and used to put delicate foods on while they are chilling or setting.

WIRE RACK

This is used to cool hot food and may be round, square or oblong. Some cakes and biscuits become soggy underneath if they are not put on a wire rack to cool.

PIPING BAG

A tough bag made of plastic or material. The bag has a pointed end with a small hole in it. You put a nozzle in the hole, then fill the bag with cream or other food. When you fold the ends of the bag together and squeeze, the food comes out in patterns.

NOZZLE

There are lots of different nozzles. Tiny nozzles are used to decorate cakes. Very big nozzles are used to pipe mashed potato into swirls. Medium sized nozzles are used for piping whipped cream on cakes.

HOW TO . . . CHOP AN ONION

Chop the ends off the onion.

Peel the onion.

Cut into thin slices.

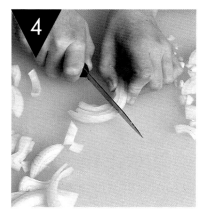

Chop the slices into small pieces.

HEATPROOF MAT

Before you take a hot pan or cooking container off the hob or from the oven, place a heatproof mat on the work surface. Put the hot pan on the mat so the work surface doesn't get scorched.

CLEAN MUSHROOMS

1 Cut off the ends of the mushroom stalks.
2 Mushrooms must not be put into a bowl of water. Rinse them 1 at a time under cold running water. Hold the mushroom like an umbrella under the water, with the stalk down and the rounded side up.
3 Rub any dirt off the rounded side with your fingers. Shake the water off the mushroom. Put the mushroom with the stalk up on double thick absorbent kitchen paper. Pat it dry.

MAKE BREADCRUMBS

1 Cut the crusts off a piece of bread.
2 Rub the bread on the coarse side of a grater, letting the crumbs fall into a bowl.
3 If you have a blender or food processor, then ask an adult if they will make some breadcrumbs for you in that.

RUB FAT INTO FLOUR

1 Use a knife to cut the fat into small pieces.
2 Wash and dry your hands in cold water. If your hands are warm the fat will become very sticky.
3 Use just the tips of your fingers to pick up a lump of fat and some flour. Lift it slightly above the mixture.
4 Rub the fat and flour together between your thumb and fingertips. Let the mixture fall back into the bowl.
5 The mixture is ready when there are not any large lumps of fat. It should look like fresh breadcrumbs.

SEPARATE AN EGG

Tap the egg in the middle to break the shell. Pull the shell lightly apart with your thumbs.

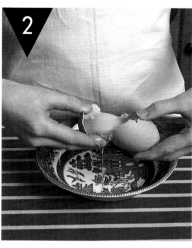

Let the white run into the basin and keep the yolk in the shell.

Open the shell into two pieces. Keep the yolk in one half.

Pour the white from each half into the basin. Tip the yolk into a second basin.

FILL A PIPING BAG

1 Put the nozzle in the piping bag.
2 Put the nozzle end of the bag in a measuring jug and fold the rest of the bag down around the outside of the jug.
3 Use a spoon to put the cream or other mixture in the bag.
4 Gather up the ends of the bag and twist them together.

PIPE CREAM

Put the nozzle in the piping bag.

Put the nozzle end in a measuring jug. Fold the bag around the jug.

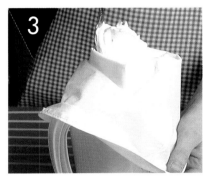

Put the cream in the bag using a spoon.

Hold the nozzle just above what you want to pipe and squeeze the bag to push out the cream.

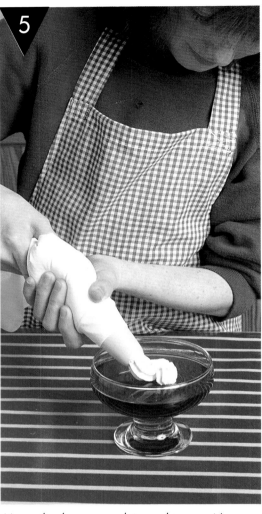

Move the bag around to make a swirl.

A NOTE TO ADULTS

The recipes in this book include some that are very simple and others that are more suitable for older children. Always supervise young children when they are cooking. Encourage your children to cook but always make sure they ask to use the kitchen so you know what they are doing. If they are preparing food that involves using the hob, oven or grill, then stay with them. No matter what age, always check what they are doing, which foods they are using, the utensils and the results.

COOKING FOR FUN

▶· Crazy Crackers ·◀

Make these using other ingredients — try using pieces of cooked ham or salami, small pieces of red or green pepper, cut up small pickled gherkins or use sliced celery sticks. Have fun making lots of different patterns or try these ideas.

12 large square cream crackers or water biscuits

Boats
2 tablespoons cream cheese
1 cheese slice
2 slices tomato
4 small sticks cucumber
4 tiny triangles cucumber peel

Faces
½ teaspoon tomato ketchup
2 tablespoons cream cheese
a few potato sticks
8 raisins
2 radishes

Flowers
2 tablespoons cream cheese
1 tablespoon chopped parsley
1 cheese slice
a little tomato ketchup
4 slices cucumber

Makes 12

1 To make the boats, spread the cream cheese on 4 crackers and make small peaks in it to look like waves. Cut 8 small triangles out of the cheese slice to look like sails. Cut the tomato slices in half.

2 Put a piece of tomato on each cracker to look like the bottom of the boat and put the cheese triangles above the tomatoes to look like sails. Leave a little space all around the sails. Put strips of cucumber between the sails to make masts and add a small triangle of cucumber peel to look like a flag.

3 For the faces, mix the ketchup with the cream cheese and spread it on 4 crackers. Break the potato sticks and put them on the crackers to look like hair. Add 2 raisins to each to look like eyes. Cut the radishes into quarters. Put 1 piece of radish in the middle of the face to look like a nose, making sure the red skin is facing up. Turn the other wedges of radish on their sides and place on the crackers to look like mouths.

4 To make the flowers, mix the cream cheese with the parsley and spread it on 4 crackers. Use a small flower shaped biscuit cutter or small round cutter to cut 4 pieces out of the cheese. Put 1 on each cracker.

5 Cut a thin strip from the middle of each cucumber slice and put these on the crackers to look like the stem of the flower. Put the other pieces of cucumber at the bottom of the stems to look like leaves. If the cucumber is too big, cut the pieces in half.

6 Put a little tomato ketchup on a saucer. Dip a cocktail stick in the ketchup and dot it in the middle of the cheese flowers. Put lots of small dots of ketchup in each flower.

▸·*rainbow Sputnik*·◂

225 g/8 oz cheese
8 radishes
1 salami stick
1 celery stick
1 grapefruit

Dip
100 g/4 oz soft cheese with herbs and garlic
4 tablespoons mayonnaise or natural yogurt
1 tablespoon tomato ketchup

Serves 6–8

1 Cut the cheese into slices measuring about 5 mm/¼ in thick. Cut the slices into cubes, then stick a cocktail stick into each cube.

2 Cut the radishes in half. Put some of the radishes on the ends of the cocktail sticks with cheese, put others on cocktail sticks of their own.

3 Cut the salami stick into 2.5 cm/1 in pieces and put them on cocktail sticks. Cut the celery stick into 2.5 cm/1 in pieces and pierce each one with a cocktail stick.

4 Cut a very thin slice off the bottom of the grapefruit so that it sits firmly on a plate. Stick all the cocktail sticks of food into the grapefruit.

5 In a basin, mix the soft cheese with the mayonnaise or yogurt and the tomato ketchup. When the mixture is smooth put it in a small dish to serve with the Rainbow Sputnik. Each person takes a cocktail stick out of the grapefruit and dips it in the cheese mixture.

▶· Cheese Savouries ·◀

3 cream crackers or water biscuits
100 g/4 oz curd cheese
2 teaspoons tomato ketchup
2 small bags salted crisps
(pick your favourite flavour)
a few parsley sprigs

Makes 15

1 Put the biscuits or crackers in a polythene bag and lay it flat on the work surface. Fold the end of the bag under. Use a rolling pin to crush the biscuits. Do this gently, until the biscuits are all in crumbs.

2 Put the curd cheese in a basin. Use a plastic or wooden spoon to stir the cheese. Add the biscuit crumbs and stir well until the cheese and crumbs are mixed.

3 Add the ketchup and stir until it is evenly mixed with the cheese.

4 Use your fingers to crush the crisps in their packets. Do this gently so as not to burst the bags. When all the crisps are broken into little pieces, turn them out on to a large plate.

5 Wash and dry your hands. Take a teaspoonful of the cheese mixture and roll it into a ball. Do this quickly and put the ball on the crushed crisps. Roll the cheese ball in the crisps until it is covered all over.

6 Shape all the mixture into balls and place them on a plate. You may put the balls into plain paper sweet cases if you like. Gently press a tiny sprig of parsley on top of each ball.

▶· Crunch Munch ·◀

*1 orange
100 g/4 oz muesli
100 g/4 oz chocolate
a little icing sugar*

Makes 12

1 Stand a grater on a board and use the fine side to grate the rind off half the orange. Brush all the rind off the grater. Mix the rind with the muesli in a basin. Cut the orange in half and squeeze the juice from one half, then pour it over the muesli.

2 Break the chocolate into small pieces and place them in a heatproof basin. Put some water in a small saucepan and put it on the hob. Stand the basin over the pan of water and turn the heat to medium. Stir the chocolate until it has all melted. Take care not to let the water boil up in the saucepan. Turn the heat off. Use oven gloves to lift the basin off the pan.

3 Mix the melted chocolate with the muesli to coat all the little bits. Leave the mixture for a while until the chocolate is beginning to set. While you are waiting, set out 12 large paper sweet cases. Use your hands to roll the mixture into balls about the size of a walnut.

4 Put the balls in the paper cases. Put a small spoonful of icing sugar in a tea strainer or small sieve and sprinkle a little sugar on top. Leave to set in a cool place.

▶· Clever Cookies ·◀

24 plain sweet biscuits
jam or chocolate spread
175 g/6 oz icing sugar
1–2 tablespoons water

Decoration
coloured sugar strands
chocolate buttons
a few glacé cherries
mimosa balls
angelica

Makes 12

1. Spread 12 biscuits with jam or chocolate spread and press the other biscuits on top.

2. Sift the icing sugar into a basin. Add 1 tablespoon of the water and mix it with the sugar, adding some or all of the remaining water to make a smooth icing. The icing must not be too runny.

3. Use a teaspoon to put some icing in the middle of each Clever Cookie, spreading it out a little to cover the top. Set about 4 of the cookies aside to dry, then sprinkle them with sugar strands.

4. Press a ring of chocolate buttons on to 4 of the cookies while the icing is wet. Overlap the buttons neatly. Cut 2 glacé cherries in half and put half in the middle of the ring of buttons.

5. Put jellied sweets or cake decorations on the other cookies.

6. Leave the icing to set before putting the cookies on a plate.

▶· banana date logs ·◀

1 small banana
1 tablespoon icing sugar
100 g/4 oz chopped cooking dates
4 tablespoons desiccated coconut
50 g/2 oz plain sweet biscuits
4 tablespoons drinking chocolate

Makes 16

1 Peel the banana and break it into pieces. Put the pieces in a basin and use a fork to mash them. Sift in the icing sugar and mix in the dates and the desiccated coconut.

2 Put the biscuits in a polythene bag and fold the end over. Use a rolling pin to crush them into fine crumbs. Stir the crushed biscuits into the mixture.

3 Wash and dry your hands. Take small spoonfuls of the mixture and roll them into 16 balls. Flatten the balls and shape them into logs about 2.5 cm/1 in long.

4 Sprinkle the drinking chocolate on a plate. Roll the logs in the drinking chocolate to coat them completely. Put them into paper sweet cases and put them in the refrigerator for at least 30 minutes.

·jammy birthday cake·

1 bought plain cake (any type will do)
175 g / 6 oz jam (your favourite flavour)
75 g / 3 oz desiccated coconut
50 g / 2 oz multi-coloured glacé cherries
angelica
birthday candles and holders
piece of red ribbon

Makes about 10 slices

1 Place the cake on a flat plate. Use a spoon to put the jam on the top of the cake, near the middle. Scrape all the jam off the spoon with a knife.

2 Spread the jam evenly over the top of the cake, taking care that it does not fall down the side. Sprinkle the coconut all over the jam in a nice thick layer.

3 Use a small knife to cut the cherries into quarters. Cut small, thin strips of angelica.

4 Make cherry flowers on the top of the cake. Put pieces of cherry together so they look like petals and use a piece of angelica for a stalk.

5 Stick birthday candles in their holders between the cherry flowers. Use a pastry brush to brush any crumbs and bits of coconut off the plate. Tie a bow of ribbon around the side of the cake.

▶ · chocolate orange fingers · ◀

1 bought loaf cake (plain or chocolate)
4 tablespoons chocolate spread
1 tablespoon orange marmalade
white chocolate buttons
jellied orange slices

Makes 10

1 Cut the cake into 5 thick slices. Cut each slice in half through the middle to make 10 long fingers. Put the fingers on a board with the crust side of the cake upwards.

2 Put the chocolate spread in a basin and gradually beat in the marmalade, adding a spoonful at a time. Spread some of this topping over the cake fingers, making small peaks or swirls in it.

3 Press a line of white chocolate buttons on top of some of the fingers. Put some jellied orange slices on top of the other fingers. Arrange the fingers on a plate to serve.

▶·hidden cherries·◀

12 glacé cherries
225 g/8 oz marzipan
a little green food colouring
3 tablespoons caster sugar

Makes 12

1 Cut the marzipan in half. Set 1 piece aside. Stick a cocktail stick into the food colouring and dab some on the second portion of marzipan, then knead it evenly until the whole piece is pale green. If it is not green enough, dab more colouring on to it and knead it again.

2 Cut each piece of marzipan into 6 pieces. Half the pieces should be yellow, the other half should be green. Take a piece of marzipan and roll it into a ball, then flatten it on the palm of your hand. Put a cherry on the marzipan, then fold it all around the cherry to cover it completely.

3 Roll the marzipan covering into a neat ball. When all the cherries are covered in marzipan, put the sugar on a plate and roll them in it. Put the Hidden Cherries into paper sweet cases.

▶·*frosted fruit*·◀

1 lemon
50 g / 2 oz caster sugar

Choose from the following fruit:

red and green dessert apples
green and black grapes
cherries with stalks
strawberries with stalks
mandarin oranges

Frosted fruit are easy to make. You will need pieces of fruit or small whole fruit.

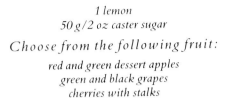

Wash the fruit. Cut the apples in half and cut out the cores. Thinly slice each piece of apple. Peel the oranges.

Squeeze the juice from the lemon and put it in a small basin.

Push a skewer into a piece of fruit. Dip it into the lemon juice.

Roll the damp fruit in a bowl of caster sugar until it is completely coated.

Put the fruit into a paper case. You can use the end of a fork to push it off the skewer.

Glacé cherries may also be coated in sugar, but they should not be dipped in lemon juice.

▶ Choc-Chip Ice Cream ◀

425 g/15 oz can custard
1 teaspoon vanilla essence
40 g/1½ oz packet dessert topping mix
150 ml/¼ pint milk
100 g/4 oz chocolate chips

Serves 6

1 Pour the custard into a bowl and stir in the vanilla. Put the dry topping mix into a basin and slowly stir in the milk. Whisk the topping mix until it is thick.

2 Add the topping mix to the custard and use a large metal spoon to fold the two together. Turn the spoon sideways to cut through the mixture, then lift a spoonful of custard over the topping. Do this until the mixture is evenly mixed. Lightly stir in the chocolate chips and pour the mixture into a freezer container.

3 Cover the container and put it in the freezer until the mixture is beginning to harden around the edges. This will take about 2 hours, possibly longer. Stir the mixture well to break up all the icy bits, then put it back in the freezer. Leave for another 2 hours, or until it is getting hard around the edges. Stir it well as before. Put it back in the freezer and leave for several hours, or overnight, until the ice cream is set.

4 Use a scoop or a spoon to serve the ice cream. If it is very hard, leave the container in the refrigerator for about 30 minutes before trying to scoop the ice cream.

IT'S SIMPLE TO START COOKING

▶·*nutty eggs*·◀

4 eggs
100 g / 4 oz cottage cheese
2 tablespoons crunchy peanut butter
salt and pepper
4 slices cucumber

Makes 8

1 Put the eggs in a small saucepan and pour in enough cold water to cover them. Put the saucepan on the hob and turn the heat to high. When the water boils, turn the heat to medium. Boil the eggs for 10 minutes.

2 While the eggs are boiling, put the cottage cheese in a basin and mash it with a fork until all the lumps are broken. The cheese should be fairly smooth.

3 Turn off the heat. Take care when lifting the saucepan off the hob. Put it in the sink and pour off the boiling water. Run cold water on to the eggs and leave them until they are cold.

4 Tap the cold eggs on the work surface to crack their shells, then pull off all the shells. This is easy if you break the very fine skin that lies just underneath the shell. Put the shelled eggs on a plate.

5 Cut the eggs in half lengthways. Use a teaspoon to scoop out the yolks. Add the yolks to the cottage cheese and mash them with it. Add the peanut butter and mash the mixture together. Stir in a little salt and pepper.

6 Use a teaspoon to put the cottage cheese mixture into the egg whites. Place the stuffed eggs on a plate. Cut the cucumber slices into quarters and stick 2 pieces into the stuffing on each egg.

▸ red hot jackets ◂

2 large potatoes
a little cooking oil
butter

Serves 4

MICROWAVE TIP
Potatoes cook quickly in the microwave. Put them on a double-thick piece of absorbent kitchen paper. Prick them in a few places with a fork. Cook them on Full Power for 12–15 minutes, rotating their positions halfway through cooking.

1 Set the oven at 200°C/400°F/gas 6. Wash the potatoes, scrubbing them with a small brush. Cut out any bad bits, then dry the potatoes on absorbent kitchen paper. Prick them in a few places and put on a baking tray.

2 Brush a little oil all over the potatoes, then bake them for 1–1¼ hours. Use oven gloves to remove the baking tray from the oven. Hold 1 potato with a clean tea-towel and carefully stick a fork into it. If the potato feels soft in the middle it is cooked. If the middle of the potato still feels hard, then it should be cooked for another 5 minutes before testing it again. Turn the heat off.

3 Hold one side of the potato with a tea-towel and cut it in half. Place on individual plates, then top each half with a knob of butter. Cut the other potato in the same way. If you like try some of the following tremendous toppings and fillings.

▸· *golden jackets* ·◂

2 baked potatoes
75 g / 3 oz cheese
200 g / 7 oz can cream-style corn
salt and pepper

1 Bake the potatoes and cut them in half following the recipe for Red Hot Jackets (page 23). Leave the oven on. Have a basin ready, then use a teaspoon to scoop the soft middle out of the potatoes and put it in the basin. Take care not to tear the potato skins.

2 Mash the potato. Grate the cheese. Stir the cheese and the cream-style corn into the potato. Stir in a little salt and pepper.

3 Use the teaspoon to put the potato mixture back into the skins. Place them on a baking tray and fork the top of the mixture into short peaks. Bake them for 10–15 minutes, until the top of the filling is lightly browned and slightly crisp.

4 Turn the heat off. Use oven gloves to take the potatoes from the oven and put them on plates.

▸· *potatoes with fishy filling* ·◂

1 Bake the potatoes and cut them in half following the recipe for Red Hot Jackets (page 23). Leave oven on. Turn the sardines and all their sauce into a basin and mash them with a fork. Use a teaspoon to scoop the middle out of the potatoes, then add it to the sardines and mash it with them. They should be well mixed. Take care not to tear the potato skins.

2 Wash and dry the spring onions. Cut off any bad bits. Use a pair of scissors to snip off the green parts of the onions in small bits. Save the white ends for a salad. Mix the green spring onion with the potato and fish, adding a little salt and pepper.

3 Use a teaspoon to put the potato mixture back into the skins. Place them on the baking tray and press the top of the filling down neatly. Grate the cheese and sprinkle a little on top of each potato. Put back in the oven for 10–15 minutes, until the cheese has melted.

4 Cut the tomato into slices. Turn the oven off. Use oven gloves to take the potatoes from the oven and put them on plates. Top each potato with a tomato slice and parsley.

2 baked potatoes
120 g / 4¼ oz can sardines in tomato sauce
2 spring onions
salt and pepper
25 g / 1 oz cheese
1 tomato
4 parsley sprigs

5

potatoes with creamy ham topping

*2 baked potatoes
100 g/4 oz soft cheese
100 g/4 oz cooked ham
salt and pepper
8 slices cucumber*

1 Bake the potatoes and cut them in half following the recipe for Red Hot Jackets (page 23). Turn the oven off.

2 Put the soft cheese in a basin. Cut the ham into slices, then cut across the slices to small dice. Mix the ham with the soft cheese. Mix in a little salt and pepper.

3 Use a teaspoon to pile the cheese and ham on top of the potatoes. Stick 2 cucumber slices into the topping on each potato and serve at once.

beany potatoes

1 Bake the potatoes and cut them in half following the recipe for Red Hot Jackets (page 23). About 5 minutes before the end of the cooking time for the potatoes, turn the baked beans into a small saucepan and put them on the hob. Turn the heat to medium. When the beans are bubbling, turn the heat down to the lowest setting.

2 Grate the cheese if you are using it. Turn the oven and hob off. Use oven gloves to take the potatoes from the oven and put them on plates. Top each potato with some of the beans. Sprinkle each one with a little grated cheese if you like.

*2 baked potatoes
225 g/8 oz can baked beans
25 g/1 oz cheese (optional)*

OTHER SIMPLE TOPPINGS FOR BAKED POTATOES

★ A spoonful of crunchy peanut butter
★ A spoonful of cottage cheese sprinkled with chopped parsley
★ A spoonful of mayonnaise mixed with a little tomato ketchup
★ A frankfurter with 6 slices of cucumber and a little mustard
★ Two slices of salami and a sliced tomato
★ A spoonful of flaked tuna fish topped with thick natural yogurt

·►· bean feast ·◄·

*2 large round crusty bread rolls
½ small onion
2 tablespoons vegetable oil
¼ teaspoon dried sage
225 g/8 oz can baked beans
50 g/2 oz cheese*

Serves 2

1 Use a sharp knife to cut a small cap off the tops of the rolls. Take care not to cut your fingers. Save the slices. Pull the soft middle out of the rolls, leaving just the crisp shells. Be careful not to break the crusts.

2 Put the soft bread on a board and cut it into small pieces. Chop the onion.

3 Put the oil in a small saucepan on the hob. Turn the heat to medium. Add the onion to the oil in the pan and cook it, stirring occasionally, for about 5 minutes, or until it is soft but not brown. Stir in the sage and bread. Cook for 5 minutes, stirring all the time.

4 Add the baked beans to the bread mixture and heat them until they are boiling. Stir the beans occasionally.

5 Grate the cheese. Turn the heat off. Take the pan off the heat and stir in the cheese with a little salt and pepper.

6 Put the bread roll shells on plates and fill them with the bean mixture. Put the roll tops on top and serve at once. A crunchy salad tastes good with these.

·►· toast toppers ·◄·

Here are some ideas for hot toast toppings. Make the topping before you toast the bread so the toast does not go cold and hard.
★ Always take great care when using the grill. Use oven gloves to handle the grill pan. Before putting food under the grill have plates ready to put it on when it is cooked. Watch the food all the time it is cooking under the grill so it doesn't burn.
★ All these toppings are for 2 pieces of toast.

FISH-TOPPED FINGERS
Put 50 g/2 oz soft cheese in a basin. Add a small pot of salmon paste. Mix them together, then stir in 1 teaspoon tomato ketchup. Spread the mixture on the toast and cook it under the grill until hot. Cut the toast into fingers and top each one with parsley.

APPLE AND CHEESE
Wash and dry 1 dessert apple. Hold the apple at both ends of the core, then grate it on the coarse side of a grater. Grate all the flesh off the apple until you reach the core. Mix 50 g/2 oz grated cheese with the apple. Use a teaspoon to put the mixture all over the toast, then cook it under the grill until the cheese has melted.

PEANUT RAREBIT
In a basin mix 2 tablespoons crunchy peanut butter with 2 tablespoons milk. When the peanut butter is very soft mix in 50 g/2 oz grated cheese and add a little salt and pepper. Spread this over the toast. Cook under the grill until bubbling.

PIZZA TOPPING
In a small basin mix 25 g/1 oz softened butter or margarine with 1 tablespoon tomato purée and ¼ teaspoon dried marjoram. Mix in a little salt and pepper. Spread the tomato mixture on the toast. Top each slice of toast with a slice of cheese. Cook the cheese under the grill until bubbling.

►·Coleslaw Cups·◄

Salads are easy to make and they can taste really scrummy!

100 g/4 oz white cabbage
1 small onion
1 large carrot
1 eating apple
1 tablespoon crunchy peanut butter
6 tablespoons mayonnaise
salt and pepper
4 large lettuce leaves

Serves 4

1 You will need a large board and a sharp knife. Cut any large pieces of stalk off the cabbage. Cut across the cabbage leaves into thin slices. The slices should fall apart into shreds.

2 Peel and chop the onion. Wash and dry the apple, then cut it into quarters. Cut out the core from each portion of apple. Cut across each apple quarter to make small, thin slices. Trim the ends off the carrot and peel or scrub it, then grate it on the coarse side of a grater.

3 Mix the cabbage, onion, apple and carrot together in a bowl. Put the peanut butter in a small basin and gradually mix in the mayonnaise. Add a little salt and pepper. Add the peanut mixture to the salad. Use a spoon and fork to mix the dressing into the salad.

4 Wash the lettuce leaves and dry them on absorbent kitchen paper. Put the leaves on a plate and pile the salad into them.

·►·Sesame Cheese Puffs·◄·

*75 g/3 oz cheese
2 tablespoons sage and onion stuffing mix
plain flour for rolling out pastry
100 g/4 oz puff pastry, thawed if frozen
a little milk or beaten egg
1 tablespoon sesame seeds*

Makes 8

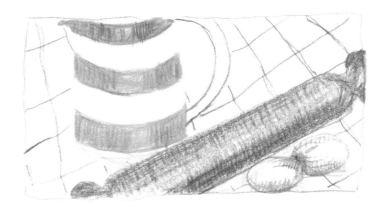

1 Grate the cheese. In a basin, mix the cheese with the stuffing mix. Set the oven at 230°C/450°F/gas 8. Have a baking tray ready – there is no need to grease it for these pastries.

2 Sprinkle a little flour on the work surface, then roll out the pastry into a 20 cm/8 in square. Only roll the pastry out away from you and do not press too hard. Press the edges of the pastry into shape with your fingers every now and then to make sure it stays square as you roll it.

3 Sprinkle the cheese mixture over half the pastry, leaving a narrow border all around the edge. Brush this border with a little water. Fold the other half of the pastry over the cheese filling and press it down firmly all over. Press the edges together.

4 Cut the pastry across into 2.5 cm/1 in wide strips. Press each strip together firmly to hold in the filling, then put them on the baking tray. Brush the top of each strip carefully with a little milk or egg. Sprinkle a few sesame seeds on top of each strip.

5 Bake the strips for 7–10 minutes. While they are baking, set out a wire rack and put a heatproof mat on the work surface. Open the oven to have a look. The pastry strips should be puffed up and golden brown. Turn the oven off. Use oven gloves to lift the baking tray from the oven. Take great care not to burn yourself.

6 Put the baking tray on the mat. Use a palette knife or fish slice to life the Sesame Cheese Puffs off the baking tray and put them on the wire rack to cool.

►·crunchy hot orange·◄

2 chocolate chip cookies
1 orange
½ teaspoon honey
2 tablespoons
natural yogurt

Serves 2

Place the cookies in a polythene bag and use a rolling pin to crush them. Do not break them too much.

Cut a very small slice of peel off the top and bottom of the orange. Cut the orange in half.

Use a small knife to cut between the orange segments and cut all around the inside of the skin so that the fruit comes out easily.

Place the orange on a baking tray and spoon on a little honey. Put them under the grill for 2–3 minutes until they are hot.

Pile the crushed biscuits on top of the oranges.

Decorate each with a spoonful of yogurt.

·nutty fruit salad·

You can use all sorts of fresh fruit in a fruit salad. For a special occasion you may be able to add some of the more expensive exotic fruit. Remember that all stones, cores and pips must be removed before the fruit is mixed in the salad. If you cannot eat the peel on the fruit, then you must cut that off, too. Try to cut all the pieces of fruit to about the same size.

*25 g/1 oz sultanas
2 oranges
50 g/2 oz grapes
a little lemon juice
1 red apple
1 green apple
2 bananas
2 tablespoons clear honey
50 g/2 oz chopped nuts
(toasted hazelnuts, mixed nuts or almonds)*

Serves 4

1 Put the sultanas in a mug. Cut 1 orange in half and squeeze out all the juice from both halves. Pour the juice over the sultanas and set them aside.

2 Cut a thin slice off the bottom of the other orange. Stand it firmly on the board and cut off all the peel and pith in strips from the top to the bottom of the orange. Take care not to cut off any of the fruit. Cut the orange into slices. Pick out all the pips, then cut each slice into 4 pieces. Put the orange in a salad bowl.

3 Cut all the grapes in half and pick out any pips. Add the grapes to the orange. Put the lemon juice in a small basin. Cut the apples into quarters. Cut the core from each apple quarter, then cut each quarter into 3 chunks. Dip the chunks of apple in the lemon juice before adding them to the orange.

4 Peel the bananas and cut them into thick slices. Dip the slices in any leftover lemon juice, then add them to the salad. Trickle the honey over the fruit. Pour the sultanas and orange juice into the salad. Mix the salad without breaking up the fruit. If not serving at once, cover with cling film and place in the refrigerator. Sprinkle the nuts over the top just before serving.

▶· Simple Scones ·◀

225 g/8 oz plain flour
3 teaspoons baking powder
50 g/2 oz margarine
2 tablespoons caster sugar
150 ml/¼ pint milk
extra plain flour
milk for brushing

Makes 12

DIFFERENT SORTS OF SCONES

★ Add 50 g/2 oz sultanas or raisins with the sugar.
★ Add 50 g/2 oz chopped walnuts with the sugar.
★ Do not add the sugar. Instead, add 50 g/2 oz grated cheese after you have rubbed in the margarine to make Cheese Scones.
★ Do not add the sugar. Instead, add 50 g/2 oz grated cheese and ½ teaspoon dried mixed herbs after you have rubbed in the margarine to make Cheese and Herb Scones.
★ Scones with cheese added may have a little grated cheese sprinkled on top before baking.

1 Set the oven at 220°C/425°F/gas 7. Grease a baking tray. Put the flour in a bowl and stir in the baking powder. Add the margarine. Rub the fat into the flour until the mixture resembles fine breadcrumbs.

2 Stir in the sugar. Make a well in the middle of the mixture. Pour the milk into the well and stir the flour into it until you have a soft dough.

3 Sprinkle some flour on the work surface and turn the dough on to it. Sprinkle just a little flour on your fingers, then gently knead the dough into a ball.

4 Use a rolling pin sprinkled with a little flour to roll the dough out until it is 1.5 cm/¾ in thick. Use a round pastry cutter measuring about 5 cm/2 in across. Dip it in a little flour, then cut out rounds of dough. Gather up all the scraps of dough and roll them out to cut out more scones.

5 Put the scones on the baking tray. Brush their tops with a little milk and bake them for 7–10 minutes. While they are cooking put a wire rack ready. Put a heatproof mat on the work surface.

6 Turn off the heat. Use oven gloves to take the scones from the oven, then use a fish slice to lift them on to the rack. Eat the scones warm, with some butter and jam.

▸ orange flapjacks ◂

*1 orange
100 g/4 oz margarine
4 tablespoons golden syrup
2 tablespoons demerara sugar
225 g/8 oz rolled oats*

Makes 16

1 Set the oven at 190°C/375°F/gas 5. Grease a 20 cm/8 in square tin really well. Grate the rind from the orange and put it in a small saucepan.

2 Add the margarine and syrup to the orange rind. Put the saucepan on the hob and turn the heat to medium. Stir the mixture in the pan until all the butter has melted. Turn the heat off.

3 Put the rolled oats in a bowl. Pour the melted mixture over the oats and mix them really well. Turn the mixture into the tin and press it down firmly until the top is smooth and even.

4 Bake the mixture for 30–35 minutes, until it is golden brown and firm. Put a heatproof mat on the work surface. Use oven gloves to remove the flapjacks from the oven.

5 Leave the mixture in the tin on the mat. When it is just warm, cut it into 16 square pieces. Leave them in the tin until they are cold and firm. Use a palette knife to remove the flapjacks.

▸ brownies ◂

1 Set the oven at 180°C/350°F/gas 4. Lay a piece of greaseproof paper on the work surface and stand a 20 cm/8 in square tin on it. Use a pencil to draw around the bottom of the tin. Cut out the paper along your pencil line. Grease the tin well. Put the square of paper in the bottom of the tin, then grease the paper.

2 Put the flour, cocoa, baking powder and sugar in a bowl and mix well. Add the margarine, eggs and vanilla essence. Stir all the ingredients into a smooth, soft mixture. Use a spoon to put the mixture into the tin and scrape the bowl clean. Spread the mixture out evenly.

3 Bake the Brownies for 40–45 minutes, until risen and the edges have come away from the tin. Put a heatproof mat on the work surface. Use oven gloves to remove the tin from the oven. Leave the Brownies in the tin on the mat until cold. Cut into 16 squares.

*75 g/3 oz self-raising flour
25 g/1 oz cocoa powder
½ teaspoon baking powder
100 g/4 oz soft brown sugar
75 g/3 oz soft margarine
2 eggs
1 teaspoon vanilla essence*

Makes 16

▸·banana muffins·◂

100 g/4 oz plain flour
2 teaspoons baking powder
50 g/2 oz sugar
25 g/1oz raisins
1 banana
25 g/1 oz soft margarine
1 egg
6 tablespoons milk

Makes 9

MUFFIN MANIA

You can add other ingredients to banana muffins:

★ *Add 50 g/2 oz roughly chopped walnuts.*
★ *Add 25 g/1 oz chopped ready-to-eat dried apricots.*
★ *Add 2 tablespoons peanut butter with the margarine.*

1 Set the oven at 200°C/400°F/gas 6. Grease 9 deep muffin tins or put 9 deep paper cake cases in patty tins. Mix the flour, baking powder, sugar and raisins in a bowl.

2 Peel the banana, break it into pieces and put them in a basin. Mash the banana with a fork until it is smooth, then add it to the dry ingredients.

3 Add the margarine and egg. Use a wooden spoon to mix all the ingredients. Add about half the milk and beat well. Beat in the remaining milk.

4 Use a teaspoon to put the mixture into the tins or paper cases, dividing it evenly. Bake the muffins for 20–25 minutes, until they are risen and golden brown. They will rise into peaks and crack slightly.

5 While the muffins are cooking, get out a wire rack and put a heatproof mat on the work surface. Turn off the heat. Use oven gloves to remove the muffins. Use a palette knife to take the muffins from their tins. Leave them to cool and eat them while they are warm.

REAL MEALS

Menu
Pronto Pasta
Exotic Jelly

1 Make the Exotic Jelly several hours before the meal or make it the day before.
2 Prepare all the ingredients for the pasta.
3 Cook the pasta and mix it with the ingredients when you are ready to eat.

ꞏ►ꞏ *pronto pasta* ꞏ◄ꞏ

1 onion
2 tablespoons vegetable oil
100 g / 4 oz mushrooms
½ teaspoon dried mixed herbs
400 g / 14 oz can choppped tomatoes
salt and pepper
4 frankfurters
350 g / 12 oz pasta shapes
50 g / 2 oz cheese
2 tablespoons chopped parsley

Serves 4

1 Peel and chop the onion. Put the oil in a saucepan over medium heat. Add the onion and cook, stirring occasionally, for about 10 minutes. The onion should be very soft but not browned.

2 While the onion is cooking, cut the end off each mushroom stalk. Rinse the mushrooms under running water, holding the round top up. Rub off any dirt. Slice the mushrooms. Add them to the onion and stir in the dried herbs. Add the tomatoes and bring the mixture to the boil. Sprinkle a little salt and pepper into the sauce. Turn the heat to the lowest setting. Slice the frankfurters and stir them into the sauce. Continue cooking, uncovered, and stir once in a while.

3 Grate the cheese and set aside.

4 You will need a large saucepan full of water to cook the pasta. Put it on the hob. Add a little salt and bring the water to the boil. When the water is boiling add the pasta. Stir the pasta once. Bring the water back to the boil but be ready to turn the heat down so that it does not boil over. The pasta should boil without frothing over the edge of the pan. Cook it like this for 15 minutes.

5 Put a colander in the sink. Turn the heat off. Use oven gloves and lift the pan of pasta from the hob, then turn it into the colander to drain. Put the pasta in a large dish. Turn the heat off under the sauce, then stir it and pour it over the pasta. Sprinkle with the cheese and parsley and serve at once. Use a spoon and fork to mix the pasta and sauce together before putting it on to plates.

exotic jelly

2 tablespoons water
3 teaspoons powdered gelatine
600 ml / 1 pint tropical fruit juice
2 tablespoons desiccated coconut
300 ml / ½ pint Greek-style yogurt
1 tablespoon clear honey
4 orange slices
biscuits, to serve

Serves 4

1 Put the water in a basin and sprinkle the gelatine over it. Do not stir it. Leave the gelatine for 15 minutes. Pour some water into a small saucepan and put it on the hob. Turn the heat on to low. Put the basin over the hot water, then stir the gelatine until it has dissolved completely. It will be clear.

2 Stir the dissolved gelatine into the tropical fruit juice. Divide this mixture between 4 glass bowls and put them in the refrigerator for at least 3 hours until set.

3 Put a piece of foil on the grill pan and spread the coconut over it. Turn the grill to a medium setting, then cook the coconut until it is golden. Stir the coconut occasionally with a long-handled wooden spoon so it browns evenly. Turn the grill off and set the coconut aside to cool.

4 Stir the yogurt with the honey. Swirl the sweetened yogurt all over the set jellies. Sprinkle the coconut over the tops. Cut the orange slices in half and put 2 pieces on each dessert. Serve your favourite biscuits with the jellies.

JELLY MAKERS

You can make other fruit jellies by using different types of fruit juice. Try orange, pineapple or apple. To make a creamy fruit jelly, use fruit-flavoured yogurt drink instead of the juice.

HELP POINT
Take great care when handling large saucepans of boiling or hot water. Always make sure there is an adult with you and ask them to lift the saucepan of boiling water to drain the pasta. Always use oven gloves when taking big pans that are hot off the hob.

CHOPPING PARSLEY

Wash a few sprigs of parsley and break off the stalks. Dry the sprigs on a piece of absorbent kitchen paper and put them in a mug. Using the point of a pair of scissors, snip at the parsley in the mug until it is all cut into small pieces. Keep the point of the scissors down in the mug to avoid spilling parsley.

Menu
Pizza
Salad Spectacular
Chocolate Yogurt Swirl

ORDER OF WORK

1 Make the Chocolate Yogurt Swirl in advance and put it in the refrigerator.
2 Collect all the ingredients for the pizza and for the salad. Wash the salad ingredients and set them aside in the refrigerator so they stay crisp.
3 Make the pizza.
4 Make the salad while the pizza is baking.

▸·*p*izza ·◂

1 onion
1 green pepper
2 tablespoons vegetable oil
4 tablespoons tomato purée
1 teaspoon dried marjoram
salt and pepper
100 g / 4 oz self-raising flour
25 g / 1 oz margarine
50 ml / 2 fl oz milk
a little flour
50 g / 2 oz frozen sweetcorn, peas or mixed vegetables
100 g / 4 oz cheese
50 g / 2 oz cooked ham

Serves 4

1 Peel and chop the onion. Cut the green pepper in half. Use a small pointed knife to cut out all the seeds and the core from each half. Cut off all the stalk from each half. Cut 1 piece of pepper into long strips, then hold all the strips together and cut across them to make small dice. Repeat with the other half.

2 Put the oil in a small saucepan. Put it on the hob and turn the heat to medium. Add the onion and diced pepper after a few seconds. Cook, stirring, for 5 minutes. Take it off the heat. Stir in the tomato purée, dried marjoram and a little seasoning. Leave to cool.

3 Grease a baking tray. Set the oven at 220°C/425°F/gas 7. Put the flour in a bowl and add the margarine. Cut the margarine into small pieces. Wash your hands, then rub the fat into the flour. Mix in the milk to make a dough and press it together with your fingers.

4 Put a little flour on the work surface and turn the dough on to it. Knead it lightly into a smooth ball. Put a little flour on a rolling pin, then roll out the dough into a circle about 20 cm/8 in across. Put the rolling pin near the middle of the dough, then fold the dough over it. Use the rolling pin to lift to the baking tray. Spread the onion mixture over the dough, leaving a small border all around the edge. Sprinkle the vegetables over the onion. Grate the cheese on the coarse side of the grater, then sprinkle it over the vegetables.

5 Cut the ham into thin strips. Place the strips in a crisscross pattern across the top of the pizza. Bake the pizza for about 15 minutes, until it is risen, bubbling and golden on top. Put a heatproof mat on the work surface. Turn the heat off. Use oven gloves to take the pizza from the oven. Cut it into wedges to serve.

►·Salad Spectacular·◄

2 carrots
2 sticks celery
4 spring onions
4 tomatoes
1 courgette
1 lettuce heart
2 tablespoons olive or sunflower oil
1 tablespoon lemon juice

Serves 4

1 Peel the carrots and cut off their ends. Grate them on the coarse side of the grater. Put them on a plate. Wash the celery and use a brush to scrub all the dirt from inside the sticks. Cut across the sticks to make thin slices. Put the celery beside the carrots on the plate, keeping both separate.

2 Wash and trim the ends off the spring onions. Peel away any bad bits. Cut the onions across into small pieces. Push them to one side of the board or put them on a plate. Cut the tomatoes into quarters.

3 Wash and dry the courgette. Cut off the ends, then cut the courgette in half lengthways. Put the cut side of a half down on the board, then cut it into thin slices. Slice the other half in the same way.

SALAD IDEAS

You can use different vegetables to make this salad. Make sure they are all cut up into small, neat pieces. Try white or red cabbage, cucumber, watercress, mushrooms or cauliflower. Add some crunchy beansprouts, too.

4 Wash and dry the lettuce. Use your fingers to tear the leaves into small pieces. You will need a large platter for the salad. Arrange all the vegetables in neat mounds coming from the centre of the platter out to the edge. Very carefully trickle the oil all over the salad, then trickle the lemon juice over.

►·Chocolate Yogurt Swirl·◄

100 g/4 oz chocolate
25 g/1 oz butter
2 tablespoons golden syrup
4 150 g/5 oz pots of fruit yogurt or 1 450 g/1 lb tub
2 tablespoons chopped nuts

Serves 4

1 Break the chocolate into squares and put them in a heatproof basin. Add the butter and the syrup. Pour some water into a small saucepan and put it on the hob over medium heat. Stand the basin in the pan over the water. Heat the mixture until the chocolate melts, stirring occasionally. Make sure that the water does not boil up underneath the basin. Turn the heat down to low if the water begins to boil.

2 Turn the heat off and use a tea-towel or oven gloves to lift the basin off the water. Set the chocolate mixture aside until it is cool. Pour the yogurt into 4 dishes. Use a spoon to swirl the chocolate mixture through the yogurt. Put the dishes in the refrigerator until you are ready to serve them. Sprinkle the nuts over the top of the yogurt just before serving.

Menu
Tuna Crunch
Rainbow Veg
Marmalade Pears

1 Prepare the Tuna Crunch, then put it in the oven 20 minutes before you want to eat.
2 Prepare the pears and toss them in lemon juice. Leave them covered in the refrigerator until after you have finished eating the main course.
3 Prepare the vegetables for Rainbow Veg and cook them on the hob while Tuna Crunch is in the oven.

▸· tuna Crunch ·◂

1 Set the oven at 190°C/375°F/gas 5. Peel and chop the onion. Open the can of tuna. Holding the lid in place, drain the oil from the can into a small saucepan. Add the onion to the oil and put the pan on the hob. Turn the heat to medium and cook the onion, stirring, for about 10 minutes, or until it is soft.

2 Turn the heat to the lowest setting. Add the flour to the onion and stir so that it makes a paste with the oil. Add just a little of the milk and stir it into the paste. Add more milk and stir it in. Continue adding the milk, a little at a time, stirring all the time. Cook the sauce, stirring, until it boils. Turn off the heat.

3 Add the tuna from the can. Break the fish into pieces when it is in the sauce. Stir in a little salt and pepper. Rinse the mushrooms under cold water, rubbing off any dirt, then cut them into slices. Add the mushroom slices to the tuna mixture.

4 Grate the cheese on the coarse side of the grater. Add half to the tuna and stir it in. Turn the tuna mixture into an ovenproof dish.

1 onion
200 g/7 oz can tuna in oil
25 g/1 oz plain flour
450 ml/¾ pint milk
salt and pepper
100 g/4 oz mushrooms
75 g/3 oz cheese
4 thin slices bread
1 small packet salted crisps
25 g/1 oz butter or margarine
parsley sprigs, to garnish

Serves 4

5 Cut the bread into small cubes and put them in a basin. Add the remaining cheese. Gently crush the crisps in their packet, taking care not to burst the bag. Tip the crisps into the basin and mix them with the bread and cheese. Use a spoon to sprinkle the bread mixture all over the top of the tuna mixture. Put small dots of the butter over the top.

6 Bake the Tuna Crunch for 15–20 minutes, until the cheese has melted and the bread is crisp and brown on top. Use oven gloves to lift the dish from the oven, then put it on a heatproof mat. Garnish the top with sprigs of parsley and serve.

▶·rainbow veg·◀

2 carrots
salt and pepper
2 courgettes
50 g / 2 oz frozen sweetcorn or peas
a little butter or margarine

Serves 4

1 Peel the carrots and cut off their ends. Cut them in half lengthways. Cut each piece in half again, then across into small dice. Put the carrots in a saucepan and pour in a little water to just cover them. Add a pinch of salt.

2 Wash the courgettes and cut off their ends. Cut them into thin slices. Put the carrots on the hob and turn on the heat to high. When the water is boiling add the frozen sweetcorn or peas. Leave the heat on high until the water boils, then turn it down to medium so it is just bubbling, or simmering.

3 Cook the carrots and sweetcorn for 10 minutes. Add the courgettes to the other vegetables and cook for just 2 minutes. The courgettes should be hot but not soggy. Put a colander in the sink. Turn the heat off, then drain the vegetables in the colander. Put them in a serving dish and dot with some butter or margarine, adding a sprinkling of pepper.

▶·marmalade pears·◀

4 firm pears
2 tablespoons lemon juice
1 orange
4 tablespoons orange marmalade
cream, natural yogurt or ice cream, to serve

Serves 4

HELP POINT
When making a sauce, it is easier to ask an adult to pour in the milk slowly while you stir the paste all the time.

1 Remove the stalks from the pears and peel them thinly. Cut them into quarters, then cut the core out of each piece of pear. Cut the quarters into chunks and place them in a basin. Spoon the lemon juice over and mix it into the pears. The lemon juice will stop the pears from turning brown. Cover the basin and put the pears in the refrigerator until you are ready to serve them.

2 Grate the rind from the orange on the fine side of the grater. Put the rind in a small saucepan. Add the marmalade. Set a sieve over the saucepan. Cut the orange in half and squeeze the juice from both halves through the sieve. Put the saucepan on the hob. Turn on the heat to low and stir the mixture until the marmalade has melted. Turn the heat off.

3 Put the pears into individual bowls and spoon some of the marmalade sauce over each portion. Spoon a little cream, natural yogurt or ice cream on top and serve at once.

Menu
Pork 'n' Potato Loaf
Stir-fry Vegetables
Banana Splits

ORDER OF WORK

1 Make the jam sauce for the Banana Splits.
2 Make the Pork 'n' Potato Loaf.
3 Prepare the vegetables while the Pork 'n' Potato Loaf is cooking.
4 Stir-fry the vegetables as soon as the Pork 'n' Potato Loaf is removed from the oven.
5 Make the Banana Splits just before you are ready to eat them.

▶·pork 'n' potato loaf·◀

500 g/1 lb lean minced pork
1 onion
1 teaspoon dried sage
salt and pepper
2 small eggs
500 g/1 lb potatoes
4 tablespoons plain flour
1 tomato
a few parsley sprigs

Serves 4

1 You will need a 500 g/1 lb loaf tin and a piece of greaseproof paper. Stand the tin on the paper and draw all around it with a pencil. Cut out the shape. Grease the tin and put the paper in it. Grease the paper. Set the oven at 190°C/375°F/gas 5.

2 Put the meat in a bowl. Peel the onion, then grate it on the coarse side of the grater. Take care not to grate your fingers. Cut the last little piece up very small. Add the onion to the meat. Mix in the sage with plenty of salt and pepper. Break 1 egg into a cup, then tip it into the basin and mix it well with the meat.

3 Peel the potatoes. Wash and dry them. Grate them on the coarse side of the grater. Squeeze the grated potato, then put it in another basin. Break the second egg into a cup, then tip it into the potato. Add the flour and plenty of salt and pepper. Mix well.

4 Put half the potato mixture into the tin and press it down with the back of a spoon. Put all the meat mixture on top, pressing it down so that it is smooth. Put the remaining potato mixture into the tin and spread it out evenly. Bake the loaf for 1¼ hours, until it is brown and crisp on top.

5 Have a heatproof mat ready for the tin. Use oven gloves to remove the tin from the oven. Turn the oven off. Put a plate upside down on the tin. Use oven gloves to hold them, then turn the tin upside down on to the plate. Lift the tin off. Peel the paper off the loaf.

6 Cut the tomato into slices and arrange them on top of the loaf. Add some parsley sprigs. Cut the loaf into slices to serve.

Stir-fry vegetables

1 leek
4 sticks celery
1 red pepper
225 g/8 oz green cabbage
3 tablespoons vegetable oil
salt and pepper

Serves 4

HELP POINT
Turning hot food out on to a serving plate is difficult so always ask an adult to help.

Trim the ends off the leek. Cut in half lengthways, then wash both pieces under cold running water to get rid of all the grit. Drain off the water, then cut both pieces into thin slices. *1*

Wash the celery, scrubbing off all the dirt. Cut the sticks into thin slices. Cut the pepper in half. Cut out the stalk and the core with all the seeds. Rinse both halves under running water. Cut the pieces in half lengthways, then across into short thin strips. *2*

Cut any large pieces of stalk from the cabbage. Cut across the leaves to give fine slices that fall into shreds as they are cut. Put the cabbage in a colander and wash it under cold water. Leave to drain. *3*

Put the oil in a large frying pan or wok. Put it on the hob and turn the heat to high. Add the leeks, celery and red pepper. Cook the vegetables for 3 minutes, stirring all the time. *4*

Add the cabbage and sprinkle in a little salt and pepper. Continue stirring the vegetables. Reduce the heat to medium and cook for another 5 minutes, stirring all the time. Turn off the heat and serve at once. *5*

STIR-FRY SPECIALS

Lots of different vegetables may be stir-fried. Try sliced onion, small baby sweet corn, sliced French beans, beansprouts, small pieces of cauliflower, sliced Brussels sprouts, sliced spring onions or mushrooms.

banana splits

100 g/4 oz jam
3 tablespoons orange juice
4 small bananas
8 small scoops vanilla ice cream
8–12 strawberries (optional)

Serves 4

Put the jam in a basin. Pour some water into a small saucepan and put it on the hob. Stand the basin over the water and turn the heat to medium. Stir the jam until it has melted. Turn the heat off and use oven gloves to lift the basin off the saucepan. *1*

Stir the orange juice into the jam, then leave it until cold. Peel the bananas and cut them in half lengthways. Put the 2 halves slightly apart on plates. *2*

Put 2 scoops of ice cream between each pair of banana halves. Use a teaspoon to trickle the jam sauce over the top. Add 2 or 3 strawberries to each Banana Split if you like and serve at once. *3*

ORDER OF WORK

1 Prepare the fruit for the dessert.
2 Make the Rainbow Rice.
3 Finish the Doughnut Desserts while the Rice is cooking and put them in the refrigerator or in a cool place.

Menu
Rainbow Rice
Doughnut Dessert

·rainbow rice·

1 Peel the onion and cut it in half. Cut both halves into thin slices. Peel the carrot and cut off its ends. Cut it in half lengthways, then across into slices. Scrub the celery under running water. Cut the sticks across into slices.

2 Cut the bacon rashers across into thin strips. Pour the oil into a saucepan and put it on the hob. Turn the heat to medium. Add the bacon to the pan and cook, stirring, until it is just beginning to brown.

3 Add the onion, carrot and celery. Stir and cook for 5 minutes. Add the rice and marjoram, stir well and cook for 2–3 minutes.

4 Pour the stock into the pan. Do this very carefully as it will cause a lot of steam. So make sure your arm is not stretched over the pan. Add a little salt and pepper. Stir and bring it to the boil. Turn the heat down and cover the pan. Cook for 10 minutes.

5 Add the peas. Stir once and put the lid on the pan. Cook for another 15–20 minutes, until the rice has absorbed all the stock. While it is cooking, roughly chop the peanuts. Divide between 4 plates or bowls and sprinkle the peanuts and Parmesan on top. Serve at once.

1 onion
1 carrot
2 sticks celery
225 g/8 oz rindless bacon
2 tablespoons vegetable oil
225 g/8 oz long-grain brown rice
½ teaspoon dried marjoram
450 ml/¾ pint chicken stock
salt and pepper
225 g/8 oz frozen peas
50 g/2 oz salted peanuts
grated Parmesan cheese, to serve

Serves 4

CHICKEN STOCK

Stocks add flavour to cooked dishes. Chicken stock is made by boiling the bones from roast chicken with an onion, a carrot, a stick of celery and some parsley. The water must cover all the ingredients and it is cooked for at least 1 hour or up to 3 hours. The liquid is strained and when it cools it may be frozen. Instead of making stock with bones, you can buy stock cubes that are dissolved in boiling water.

doughnut dessert

100 g/4 oz raspberries
1 orange
3 tablespoons icing sugar
4 ring doughnuts

Serves 4

1 Put the raspberries in a basin. Cut a fine slice off the bottom of the orange. Stand it on a board and cut off all the peel and pith by cutting strips down the side of the orange. Take care not to cut off any fruit.

2 Cut the orange into slices and pick out all the pips. Cut the slices into small pieces. Mix them with the raspberries. Sprinkle 2 tablespoons of the icing sugar over the fruit and set aside for at least 30 minutes.

3 Put the doughnuts on individual plates. Fill the hole in the middle of the doughnuts with the raspberries and orange. Spoon any fruit juices over the tops.

4 Just before serving the dessert, put the remaining icing sugar in a tea strainer or small sieve. Sprinkle just a little over the top of the fruit in each doughnut.

FRUITY FILLINGS

Instead of the raspberries and orange, make a fruit salad (page 30) to fill the doughnuts. You can also fill the doughnuts with canned pineapple or with canned fruit pie filling.

HOW TO SPROUT BEANS

You will need some small, green mung beans and a large jam jar. Take about enough beans to fill the jar a quarter and put them in a sieve. Wash the beans under cold water, then put them in the jar and pour in water to cover them. Leave the beans to soak overnight.

Next day, drain off the water and rinse the beans. Put them back into the rinsed jar. Cover the jar with a piece of absorbent kitchen paper and put an elastic band around it. Remove the paper and rinse and drain the beans every day. In about 3 days they will have started to grow shoots. After 4–5 days the shoots will be long enough to eat. Do not let them grow too long or they will taste bitter.

Menu
Fish Finger Flan
Baked Beans
Rice Cocktails

ORDER OF WORK

1 Make the Rice Cocktails and put them in the refrigerator.
2 Make the Fish Finger Flan.
3 Heat the baked beans 5 minutes before the end of the cooking time for the flan.

·▶· *fish finger flan* ·◀·

175 g/6 oz plain flour
75 g/3 oz margarine
1–2 tablespoons cold water
75 g/3 oz cheese
4 spring onions
2 eggs
150 ml/¼ pint milk
salt and pepper
6 frozen fish fingers
parsley sprig

Serves 6

1 Set the oven at 190°C/375°F/gas 5. Put the flour in a basin. Add the margarine and cut it into small pieces. Using just the tips of your fingers, rub the fat into the flour. Lift the fat and flour as you rub them together, then let the bits fall back into the basin. The mixture is ready when it looks like fine breadcrumbs.

2 Add 1 tablespoon cold water and mix the pastry with a knife. If it does not form large lumps add the rest of the water. Press the pastry together into a ball.

3 Get out a 20 cm/8 in flan dish. Put a little flour on the work surface and on your rolling pin. Roll out the pastry into a circle large enough to line the flan dish. To measure the pastry, hold the dish over it. There should be enough all around the edge to come up the side of the dish.

4 Put the rolling pin on the pastry. Fold the pastry over the pin, then use the rolling pin to lift it into the flan dish. Press the pastry down into the dish. If you have any breaks in the pastry just press them together with your fingers. Roll the rolling pin over the top of the dish to cut off the extra pastry.

5 Prick the pastry all over with a fork. Put a sheet of greaseproof paper in the flan. Sprinkle some dried peas over the paper. Bake the pastry for 10 minutes. Put a heatproof mat on the work surface. Use oven gloves to lift the dish from the oven. Lift the peas and paper out of the pastry case. Reduce the oven temperature to 180°C/350°F/gas 4.

6 Grate the cheese. Cut any bad bits off the spring onions, then wash them and cut them across into small pieces. Beat the eggs with the milk, adding a little salt and pepper. Set aside.

Sprinkle the cheese all over the bottom of the flan. Scatter the spring onions over the cheese, then pour in the eggs and milk. Arrange the fish fingers in the flan like the spokes of a wheel. Bake the flan for 50–60 minutes, or until the top of the fish fingers are brown and crisp and the egg is set.

Have a heatproof mat ready to put the flan on. Use oven gloves to lift the dish from the oven. Turn the oven off. Place a sprig of parsley in the middle of the flan and serve cut wedges. This can be served hot or at room temperature.

▶· baked beans ·◀

425 g / 15 oz can baked beans

Serves 4

1 Get out a small saucepan. Open the can of beans and pour them into the pan. Put the pan on the hob and turn the heat to medium.

2 Stir the beans occasionally until they are just boiling and hot through. Turn off the heat. Serve with the Fish Finger Flan.

BEANS ON TOAST

To make Beans on Toast, toast 4 slices of bread on both sides while the beans are heating. Spread some butter or margarine on the toast, then put the slices on plates. Spoon the beans over the toast and serve at once.

▶· rice cocktails ·◀

50 g / 2 oz glacé cherries
25 g / 1 oz raisins
298 g / 10½ oz can mandarin oranges
small piece angelica
425 g / 15 oz can creamed rice pudding

Serves 4

1 Cut the cherries into quarters and put them in a small basin with the raisins. Open the can of mandarin oranges. Hold the lid in place and drain all the juice from the can into another basin. Add 2 tablespoons of the juice to the cherries and raisins. The rest of the juice may be used to make a drink.

2 Leave the cherries and raisins to soak for 30 minutes. Cut the angelica into small pieces. Open the rice pudding and put it in a bowl.

3 Add the mandarin oranges and angelica to the rice. Pour in the cherries and raisins and stir well. Divide the Rice Cocktails between 4 glass bowls. Put in the refrigerator for at least 30 minutes.

ORDER OF WORK

1 Make the Coconut Cookie Cake in advance and put it in the refrigerator.
2 Make the Sandwich Supper and leave it to soak for 30 minutes before cooking.
3 Make the Tomato Salad while the Sandwich Supper is cooking.

Menu
Sandwich Supper
Tomato Salad
Coconut Cookie Cake

⊩· Sandwich Supper ·◄

8 slices bread
75 g / 3 oz butter
1 tablespoon wholegrain mustard
4 thick slices cheese
extra butter for greasing the dish
3 eggs
300 ml / ½ pint milk
salt and pepper

Serves 4

1 Cut the crusts off the bread. Spread the slices with the butter. Spread 4 slices with mustard and lay the cheese on top. Press the remaining bread slices on top to make cheese sandwiches.

2 Grease a large ovenproof dish. Cut the sandwiches across into 4 triangular pieces. Put these small sandwiches in the dish, overlapping them to fit them all in.

3 Crack the eggs 1 by 1 into a cup, putting them into a basin when you are sure there are no bits of shell in each. Use a whisk to beat the eggs. Gradually pour in the milk and whisk again.

4 Add a little salt and pepper to the egg mixture. Then pour it slowly all over the sandwiches. Leave to soak for 30 minutes so the bread has time to absorb the egg and milk.

5 Set the oven at 180°C/350°F/gas 4. Bake the sandwiches for 40–50 minutes, until they are golden brown on top and all the egg is set.

6 Put a heatproof mat ready on the work surface. Use oven gloves to remove the dish from the oven. Turn the oven off. Serve the Sandwich Supper freshly cooked but take care when eating it – the cheese is very hot!

OTHER SANDWICH FILLINGS TO TRY

★ Ham
★ Cream cheese and spring onion
★ Cheese and peanut butter

▶· tomato salad ·◀

8 tomatoes
2 spring onions
salt and pepper
1 tablespoon vegetable oil
½ teaspoon vinegar

Serves 4

1 Cut the tomatoes in half. Cut out the core and stalk end from each half. Cut the halves into thin wedges.

2 Place the tomato wedges on a plate. Trim any bad bits from the spring onions, then wash and dry them. Cut them across into small pieces, then sprinkle them over the tomatoes.

3 Sprinkle a little salt and pepper over the tomatoes. Trickle the oil all over the salad. Sprinkle the vinegar over and serve.

▶· Coconut Cookie Cake ·◀

16 coconut cookies
2 tablespoons orange juice
300 ml / ½ pint whipping cream
1 chocolate Flake
6 glacé cherries
12 angelica leaves

Serves 6

Place the cookies on a large piece of cling film. Sprinkle orange juice over the cookies until they are moist, but not soggy.

Whisk the cream in a bowl until it stands in soft peaks. Spread a little cream on 3 cookies, press them into a stack and add another on the end.

HOW TO MAKE ANGELICA LEAVES

Cut some angelica into thin strips. Cut across the strips at an angle to make diamond shapes. Turn these on end to represent leaves.

Line the cookies up and wrap cling film completely around them. Chill the cookie cake for at least 1 hour. Turn the cookie cake on its side on a plate. Then cover it with the remaining cream, crumble the Flake over the top and add cherries with angelica leaves.

Menu
Pastacular
No-cook Chocolate Fudge Flan

ORDER OF WORK

1 Make the No-cook Chocolate Fudge Flan several hours before the meal so it has time to set.
2 Prepare all the ingredients for the pasta dish at least 1 hour before you intend to serve the meal.

▶·*p*astacular·◀

1 Trim the ends off the mushroom stalks. Rinse the mushrooms, wiping off any bits of dirt. Dry them on absorbent kitchen paper, then slice them.

2 Remove the rind from the sausage if necessary. Cut the sausage into fairly thin slices. Grate the cheese. Peel and chop the onion.

3 Three-quarters fill a large saucepan with water and put it on the hob. Add a little salt and turn the heat to high. When the water boils add the pasta and give it a stir. Stand by to turn the heat down to medium as soon as the water boils. If you leave the heat on high the water will boil over. Boil the pasta for 15 minutes. Put a colander in the sink. Turn the heat off and pour the pasta into the colander. Leave to drain.

4 Put the butter in a medium saucepan and put it on the hob. Turn the heat to medium. Add the onion to the butter and cook, stirring, for 5 minutes.

5 Add the flour to the onion and stir to make a paste. Slowly pour the milk into the pan, stirring all the time. Stir in the frozen beans. Keep stirring until the sauce boils and thickens. Once it has boiled, cook the sauce for 3 minutes.

6 Add the mushrooms to the sauce and stir in the cheese. Sprinkle in a little salt and pepper. Cook, stirring, until the cheese has melted. Do not let it boil. Taste the sauce to check whether it has enough seasoning.

7 Add the cooked pasta to the sauce, stir well and cook gently for about 5 minutes, until it is hot. The beans should be hot and lightly cooked, with a bit of crunch.

8 Heat the grill. Turn the pasta mixture into a flameproof serving dish and put it under the grill until golden brown on top. Have a heatproof mat ready. Use oven gloves to remove the dish from under the grill. Turn the heat off.

*100 g/4 oz mushrooms
350 g/12 oz smoked sausage
50 g/2 oz cheese
1 onion
225 g/8 oz pasta spirals
25 g/1 oz butter
40 g/1½ oz plain flour
600 ml/1 pint milk
salt and pepper
100 g/4 oz frozen cut green beans*

Serves 4

▸ *no-cook chocolate fudge flan* ◂

100 g/4 oz plain sweet biscuits
50 g/2 oz butter

Filling
175 g/6 oz plain cake
175 g/6 oz plain chocolate
50 g/2 oz butter
6 tablespoons golden syrup
1 tablespoon cocoa powder
100 g/4 oz cream cheese
2 tablespoons icing sugar
2 tablespoons orange juice

Serves 4–6

1 Put the biscuits in a polythene bag. Twist the end closed, then fold it over. Use a rolling pin to crush the biscuits, taking care not to break the bag.

2 Put the butter in a medium saucepan. Put the pan on the hob and turn the heat to medium. When the butter has melted, turn the heat off and tip all the biscuits into the butter. Stir well.

3 Turn the buttered biscuits into a 15 cm/6 in flan dish. Press them all over the base and up the side of the dish in a thin, even coating. Put the dish in the refrigerator to chill the biscuit mixture.

4 Put the cake in a bowl. Wash and dry your hands. Crumble the cake into small, even pieces.

5 Break the chocolate into squares and put it in a saucepan. Add the butter, syrup and cocoa. Put the pan on the hob and turn the heat to low. Stir the mixture until the butter has melted and the golden syrup is runny. Turn the heat off.

6 Pour the chocolate mixture over the cake crumbs and mix really well. Carry on mixing until every bit of cake has absorbed the chocolate. Put the chocolate cake mixture into the biscuit case and press it down evenly.

7 Put the cheese in a bowl with the icing sugar and the orange juice. Beat well until the cheese is very soft. Pile this on top of the flan and swirl it out evenly.

8 Chill the flan for at least 1 hour before serving it cut into wedges.

FAST FOODS

◀▶· frankfurter kebabs ·◀▶

2 frankfurters
4 small tomatoes
8 button mushrooms
a little oil
salt and pepper

Mustard Sauce
1 tablespoon French mustard
4 tablespoons natural yogurt or fromage frais
1 spring onion

1 Cut each frankfurter into 4 pieces. Cut the tomatoes in half. Thread 4 pieces of frankfurter, 4 mushrooms and 4 tomato halves on a long metal skewer. Thread the rest of the ingredients on another metal skewer.

2 Mix the mustard with the fromage frais or yogurt. Trim the ends off the spring onion. Wash and dry it on absorbent kitchen paper, then cut it into small pieces. Stir the spring onion into the sauce.

3 Heat the grill. Brush a little oil over the kebabs and sprinkle with a little salt and pepper. Put the kebabs under the grill for 3 minutes. Use oven gloves to hold the end of the skewers and turn the kebabs over. Cook for another 3 minutes.

4 Serve the mustard sauce with the kebabs.

SERVING IDEAS

★ *Have pitta bread with the kebabs. Warm the pitta at the bottom of the grill while you cook the kebabs. Split the bread down one side and fill it with the food off the skewers.*
★ *Arrange the kebabs on a plate of shredded lettuce.*
★ *Serve Coleslaw Cups (page 27) with the kebabs.*
★ *Heat a small can of baked beans or spaghetti in tomato sauce to go with the kebabs.*

▶·pasta cover up·◀

2 rashers rindless bacon
225 g/8 oz can pasta shapes in tomato sauce,
or spaghetti hoops in tomato sauce
25 g/1 oz cheese
1 slice bread

Serves 1

Cut the bacon rashers across into thin strips. Put them in a small saucepan. Put the pan on the hob and turn the heat to medium. Stir the bacon until the fat melts and the bacon browns.

Open the can of pasta and pour it over the bacon. Stir well. Turn the heat to low and leave the pasta to heat through until just bubbling.

Grate the cheese and put it in a basin. Cut the bread into small cubes and mix them with the cheese. Heat the grill to high.

Put the pasta into a flameproof serving dish. Sprinkle the bread and cheese all over the top. Put the pasta under the grill until the cheese has melted and the bread topping is crisp and golden. Turn the heat off.

Use oven gloves to remove the dish from under the grill, then stand it on a heatproof mat. Let the topping cool for 2–3 minutes before eating.

MICROWAVE METHOD

★ Put the bacon in a small flameproof casserole dish. Cover and cook on Full Power for 2 minutes.
★ Use oven gloves to lift the dish from the microwave. Stir the bacon and check that all the bits are cooked. Add the pasta. Stir and cover the dish.
★ Heat on Full Power for 2–3 minutes, or until the pasta is hot. Stir well. Continue as above from step 4, using the same dish.

·burger salad·

1 eating apple
1 small carrot
1 spring onion
salt and pepper
1 long Granary roll
2 lettuce leaves
1 frozen burger
4 slices cucumber

Serves 1

MICROWAVE METHOD

★ **Check the weight of the burger. Put it on a plate.**
★ **Cook on Full Power. Allow about 1½–2 minutes for a 50 g/2 oz burger. A 100 g/4 oz burger takes about 3–3½ minutes.**

1 Peel the apple. Grate all the flesh off the core on the coarse side of the grater. Put the grated apple in a basin.

2 Peel the carrot and trim off the ends. Grate it on the coarse side of the grater. Mix the carrot with the apple. Trim any bad bits off the spring onion. Wash and dry it. Cut it across into small pieces. Mix the spring onion with the salad, adding a little salt and pepper.

3 Split the roll lengthways without cutting it right through. Wash and dry the lettuce leaves. Put them in the roll. Put the salad in the roll. Heat the grill.

4 Cook the burger under the grill for 3–5 minutes. It should be well browned. Use a fish slice and a fork to turn the burger over. Cook the second side for 3–5 minutes. Turn the heat off.

5 Cut the burger across the middle in half. Put the pieces onto the salad in the roll. Add the cucumber slices.

▶· barbecue-style vegi burger ·◀

½ small onion
1 clove garlic
1 tablespoon vegetable oil
2 teaspoons demerara sugar
½ teaspoon French mustard
2 tablespoons tomato ketchup
2 tablespoons water
225 g/8 oz can baked beans in tomato sauce
1 frozen vegi burger

Serves 1

MICROWAVE METHOD

★ Mix the onion, garlic and oil in a basin. Cover and cook on Full Power for 3 minutes.
★ Stir in the other sauce ingredients and the beans. Cover and cook on Full Power for 2–3 minutes, until the beans are hot.
★ Put the vegi burger on a plate. Cook on Full Power for 2–3 minutes, until it is hot through.

1 Chop the onion. Peel the garlic clove, then cut it into small pieces. Mix the onion and garlic in a small saucepan with the oil.

2 Put the pan on the hob and turn the heat to medium. Cook, stirring occasionally, for about 8 minutes, until the onion is soft. Stir in the sugar, mustard, ketchup and water. Heat, stirring, until the mixture bubbles.

3 Add the baked beans to the barbecue sauce and stir well. Leave over low heat until the beans are hot and bubbling. Heat the grill.

4 Cook the vegi burger under the grill for 3–5 minutes, until browned. Use a fish slice and fork to turn the burger over. Cook for 3–5 minutes until the second side is browned. Turn the heat off.

5 Put the vegi-burger on a plate. Turn the hob off. Spoon some of the barbecue beans over the burger and put the remainder on the plate beside it.

⊪·chicken noodles·◂∣

1 onion
1 green pepper
100 g/4 oz mushrooms
100 g/4 oz boneless cooked chicken or ham
225 g/8 oz block Chinese egg noodles
2 tablespoons vegetable oil
2 tablespoons soy sauce
100 g/4 oz frozen mixed vegetables

Serves 2

MICROWAVE METHOD

★ Soak the noodles as described above.
★ Put the onion and pepper in a dish with the oil. Cover and cook on Full Power for 3 minutes.
★ Add all the remaining ingredients except the noodles. Mix well. Cover and cook on Full Power for 7–10 minutes. Stir once during cooking.
★ Add the noodles. Mix well and serve.

1 Peel and chop the onion. Cut the green pepper in half. Cut out the stalk, core and remove all the seeds. Cut each piece of pepper in half lengthways, then across into short, thin strips.

2 Trim the ends off the mushroom stalks. Rinse the mushrooms under running water and wipe off any dirt. Slice the mushrooms. Remove any chicken skin. Cut the chicken or ham into small dice.

3 Put the noodles in a bowl. Pour boiling water from the kettle over the noodles to cover them. Leave to stand for 5 minutes. Use oven gloves and pour the noodles into a colander in the sink and leave to drain.

4 Pour the oil into a large frying pan or wok and put it on the hob. Turn the heat to medium. Add the onion and green pepper. Cook, stirring, for 5 minutes. Add the mushrooms and chicken. Cook, stirring all the time, for 5 minutes.

5 Pour in the soy sauce and add the frozen mixed vegetables. Stir well. Cook for 7–10 minutes, stirring occasionally, until the vegetables are hot.

6 Add the noodles to the pan. Mix all the ingredients together and cook for 2 minutes to heat the noodles. Turn the heat off. Divide the noodles between 2 bowls or plates.

Chicken-corn Chowder

2 spring onions
small knob of butter or margarine
50 g/2 oz boneless cooked chicken
198 g/7 oz can cream-style corn
50 ml/2 fl oz milk
salt and pepper
a few packet croûtons

Serves 1

Cut any bad bits off the spring onions, then wash and dry them. Cut them across into small pieces. Put a small knob of butter or margarine in a small saucepan. Put the pan on the hob and turn the heat to low.

When the butter has melted, add the spring onion. Stir, then leave to cook very gently for 5 minutes. While the onion is cooking, remove any skin from the chicken. Cut the chicken into small dice.

Add the chicken to the spring onion. Stir in the cream-style corn. Pour in the milk and stir to mix. Add a little salt and pepper. Increase the heat to medium and heat the soup until it is just bubbling. Cook for 2 minutes, stirring.

Turn the heat off and pour the soup into a bowl. Sprinkle packet croûtons over the top.

hash-tash

225 g/8 oz potatoes
2 tablespoons plain flour
salt and pepper
340 g/12 oz can corned beef
200 g/7 oz can sweetcorn
1 egg
2 tablespoons vegetable oil
25 g/1 oz butter or margarine

Serves 4

Peel the potatoes, then wash and grate them on the coarse side of the grater. Squeeze all the water from the grated potato. Put it in a bowl.

Add the flour and plenty of salt and pepper. Mix the flour into the potato. Use a knife to cut the corned beef up, then add it to the potatoes. Mix the beef and potatoes together using a spoon. The corned beef is soft enough to break up as you mix.

Drain the sweetcorn, then stir it and the egg into the mixture. Put a frying pan on the hob and spoon in the oil. Turn the heat to high for 30 seconds, until the oil is hot. Turn the heat down to medium.

Add all the potato mixture to the pan and spread it out evenly. Press it down firmly all over. Put a lid or large heatproof plate on top of the pan. Cook for 15–20 minutes, until the potatoes are cooked.

Heat the grill to medium. Use oven gloves to remove the lid. Turn the hob off. Dot the butter or margarine over the top of the hash, then put the pan under the grill. Cook until the top of the hash is golden and crisp. Have a heatproof mat ready. Use oven gloves to remove the pan. Turn the grill off.

Cut the hash into wedges and use a fish slice to lift them out of the pan.

▶ Salami Stick roll-ups ◀

1. Cut the crusts off the bread. Spread a thin layer of soft cheese over both slices. Spread a little tomato ketchup over the soft cheese.

2. Cut the salami stick in half. Put one piece across the end of each slice of bread. Roll up carefully without squeezing out the cheese and ketchup. Tightly wrap a piece of cling film around each sandwich and leave for 5 minutes.

3. Peel the carrot and cut the ends off. Cut in half lengthways. Cut each half lengthways into 2 sticks. Scrub the celery sticks and cut them across in half.

4. Unwrap the roll-ups and put them on a plate with the celery and carrot sticks. Eat roll-ups and vegetable sticks together.

*2 thin slices bread
a little low-fat soft cheese
a little tomato ketchup
1 salami stick
1 small carrot
1 stick celery*

Makes 2

▶ tuna rarebit rolls ◀

1 Spread the tuna mixture thickly over the half-toasted rolls. Put them back under the grill until the topping is brown. Turn the heat off.

2 Put the rolls on plates and top each half with cucumber slices and a sprig of parsley. Take care when eating – the topping is very hot!

3 Drain the liquid from the tuna. Put the tuna in a basin. Grate the cheese and mix it with the tuna. Add the milk. Sprinkle in some salt and pepper.

4 Mix the ingredients really well so they combine to make a thick paste.

5 Heat the grill. Slice the rolls in half through the middle. Put the rolls on the rack with the cut sides down. Cook until the tops are golden. Turn the rolls over. Cook the cut sides until they are only lightly browned.

99 g / 3½ oz can tuna
50 g / 2 oz cheese
2 tablespoons milk
salt and pepper
2 round bread rolls
about 8 slices cucumber
4 parsley sprigs

Serves 2

▶ toasted sandwich ◀

1 Heat the grill. Spread a little butter or margarine on the bread slices. Sandwich the bread and cheese together, pressing them down firmly, with the unbuttered sides of the bread on the outside.

2 Put the sandwich under the grill until it is golden brown on one side. Turn the sandwich over and toast the second side. Turn the grill off and eat the sandwich while it is hot. Take care when you bite the filling – the cheese gets very hot!

TREMENDOUS TOASTED SANDWICHES

Try these fillings.
★ Cheese, thinly sliced apples and a little chopped onion.
★ Mashed canned sardines with sliced pickled cucumber.
★ Mashed tuna fish with cottage cheese.
★ A thin slice of corned beef and a spoonful of baked beans.
★ A slice of cooked turkey with 2 teaspoons of cranberry sauce.
★ A slice of cooked pork with 2 teaspoons apple sauce.
★ A cooked bacon rasher with a sliced tomato.
★ Peanut butter with sliced frankfurter.

SANDWICH TOASTERS

If you have a special electric sandwich toaster ask an adult to show you how to use it. The toaster should be heated up before the sandwiches are put in it, then they are cooked for about 3 minutes. They will be very hot.

▪▶ *taco tomato scramble* ◀▪

*a few lettuce leaves
4–6 cucumber slices
1 egg
1 tablespoon milk
salt and pepper
1 tomato
a little butter or margarine
1 taco shell
parsley sprig (optional)*

Serves 1

1 Wash and dry the lettuce leaves. Tear them into small pieces and put them on a plate with the cucumber. Crack the egg into a basin. Add the milk with a little salt and pepper. Use a whisk to beat the egg and milk together.

2 Cut the tomato in half. Place the flat side down on the board, then cut both halves across into slices. Holding the slices in place cut across them to make small pieces of tomato.

3 Have a heatproof mat ready on the work surface. Put a small knob of butter or margarine in a small saucepan. A non-stick pan is best. Put it on the hob and turn the heat to medium. When the butter melts, pour the egg into the pan. Stir it all the time over the heat until it begins to get thick and set.

4 As soon as the egg is set and creamy, remove the pan from the hob. Put the pan on the mat and turn off the heat. Add the tomato to the egg and stir lightly. Put the taco shell on the plate with the salad. Spoon the egg mixture into it. Add a sprig of parsley if you like. Eat at once.

▶· tostada toppers ·◀

1 avocado
1 lettuce heart
16 slices cucumber
4 tomatoes
4 packet tostadas
4 thin slices cooked ham
75 g/3 oz cheese

Makes 4

MICROWAVE METHOD

Place 2 tostadas on a plate and cook on Full Power for about 2 minutes, until the cheese has melted. Cook the other tostadas separately. Take care — the topping is extra hot when cooked in the microwave!

MORE TOPPERS

★ Salami, sliced tomato and sliced mozzarella cheese
★ Sliced frankfurters, sweetcorn relish and cheese
★ Mashed avocado topped with rind-less bacon rashers
★ Mashed canned sardines with onion slices and cheese

1

Cut all around the avocado. Hold both sides firmly and twist one half, then pull it off the stone. Ask an adult to help you to remove the stone. If the stone is loose it will come out easily. If not, stick the point of a knife into it and pull it out. Take great care not to stick the knife into your hand.

2

Cut both pieces of avocado in half lengthways. Peel the skin off each piece and cut the flesh into 3 slices. When you have sliced all the avocado put it on a plate and cover it with cling film.

3

Wash and dry the lettuce. Break the leaves into small pieces using your fingers. Divide the lettuce between 4 plates and put 4 cucumber slices on top of each portion. Cut the tomatoes into slices.

4

Heat the grill. Put the tostadas on the grill pan and put a slice of ham on top of each. Grate the cheese on the coarse side of the grater. Sprinkle the cheese all over the ham.

5

Put the tostadas under the grill until the cheese has melted and lightly browned. Turn the heat off. Use a slice to lift the tostadas and put one on each plate, on top of the lettuce and cucumber or beside it. Divide the tomato and avocado slices between the tostadas. Serve at once.

bacon and salad croissant

1 croissant
4 slices cucumber
1 small tomato
1 lettuce leaf
1 rasher rindless bacon

Makes 1

1 Slice the croissant in half through the middle. Arrange the cucumber slices overlapping on the bottom half of the croissant, then put it on a plate.

2 Cut the tomato into slices and put them on top of the cucumber. Wash and dry the lettuce. Break the leaf into 2 or 3 pieces, then put them on top of the tomato.

3 Put the bacon rasher in a small pan and put it on the hob. Turn the heat to medium and cook until the fat runs from the bacon and the underneath is brown. Use a fork to turn the bacon over. Cook the second side until it is browned. Turn the heat off.

4 Place the slice of bacon on top of the salad. Put the top back on the croissant. Eat at once, while the bacon is still hot and the salad is crunchy.

Sausage and apple filler

1 large Granary roll
2 tablespoons soft cheese
pinch dried sage
1 lettuce leaf
½ eating apple
1 spring onion
1 pork sausage

Makes 1

1 Slice the Granary roll in half through the middle. Spread both halves with a little cheese. Sprinkle with sage.

2 Wash and dry the lettuce leaf. Cut the core out of the apple and cut it into slices. Trim any bad bits off the spring onion, wash and dry it. Cut the spring onion into 3 pieces.

3 Put the lettuce leaf on the bottom half of the roll. Arrange the apple and spring onions on top.

4 Heat the grill. Cook the sausage until it is golden brown all over. Turn it 2 or 3 times during cooking, using a fork. Have a small plate with a piece of absorbent kitchen paper on it ready.

5 Turn the heat off. Put the sausage on the paper. Pat the fat off the sausage, then cut it at an angle into thin slices. Put these on top of the apple and onion. Put the top on the roll and eat at once.

·►·*quick soup special*·◄·

2 rashers rindless bacon
½ small onion
300 g / 10 oz can tomato soup
1 tablespoon snipped chives

Serves 1

1 Cut the bacon across into thin strips. Put them in a small saucepan. Wash the spring onion and dry it. Cut the onion into thin slices and add them to the pan.

2 Put the pan on the hob and turn the heat to medium. Cook, stirring often, until the fat runs from the bacon. Continue to cook for 5 minutes, or until the onion is softened.

3 Open the can of soup and pour it into the pan. Stir and heat gently until the soup is just boiling. Turn the heat off.

4 Pour the soup into a bowl and sprinkle with the chives. Eat at once – but remember it is very hot!

MICROWAVE METHOD

Put the bacon and onion in a dish. Cover and cook on Full Power for 4 minutes. Stir the mixture twice during cooking. The bacon must be cooked. Add the soup and heat, without a cover on the dish, on Full Power for 2 minutes. Stir the soup halfway through cooking and again before you pour it into a bowl.

THROWING A PARTY

PACK UP A PICNIC

When the weather is fine, invite a few of your friends to go on a picnic. If you are asking more than your Mum and Dad can take in their car, ask your friends' parents to come along, too.

Write out invitations on pieces of coloured paper.

Picnic Party

Please come to my picnic on
Saturday 10th August at Bramble Common.
We will be at the car park at 2.00 pm.
Please bring something to sit on.
Love
Jamie

Make sure that all the parents know about the picnic and where to meet.

WHAT TO TAKE

★ A plastic sheet to put on the ground
★ Rugs to sit on
★ Plenty of paper napkins or kitchen roll
★ A paper tablecloth
★ Paper or plastic plates and mugs
★ 1 or 2 huge plastic bags to put all your rubbish in

WHAT TO PLAN

★ Food – take food that is easy to pack and to eat. Try the picnic menu or make your favourite goodies.
★ Games – plan 2 or 3 games that everyone can play together outside, such as a three-legged race. Pack anything you need to play.
★ Prizes – pack a prize for each game. Ask an adult for help with this.
★ Fun pack – plan a small fun pack for each of your guests. For example, include a balloon with a piece of string and a whistle or a toy that unrolls and squeaks when you blow it. Add a

small pack of Iced Diamond Biscuits or a fruity bar.

DO NOT

★ Let anyone wander off. Everyone has to stay together and join in the games.
★ Leave any litter. Make clearing up a fun activity at the end of the party. Give a little prize for the person who collects the most rubbish.

Picnic Menu
Mini Meatballs
Pizza Sticks
Cheese Savouries (page 13)
Sandwich Rolls
Mini Flans
Orange Flapjacks (page 32)
Brownies (page 32)

▶· *mini* *M*eatballs ·◀

*1 onion
500 g / 1 lb sausagemeat
2 tablespoons crunchy peanut butter
75 g / 3 oz fresh breadcrumbs
1 small egg
salt and pepper
1 teaspoon dried sage*

Makes about 30

Peel the onion and grate it on the coarse side of the grater. Cut up the last bit very small.

Put the onion in a basin with the sausagemeat, peanut butter and breadcrumbs. Break an egg into a cup and tip it into the bowl.

Mix the ingredients together. Break the sausagemeat up with the edge of spoon, then pound all the other ingredients into it by pressing with the back of a spoon.

Wet your hands and roll a lump of mixture into a ball about the size of a walnut.

Put these balls in a large frying pan on the hob and turn the heat to medium. When the meatballs begin to sizzle, move them around the pan as they cook until they are brown all over. Put them on a double thick piece of kitchen paper on a plate to cool.

Sandwich rolls

3 eggs
2 tablespoons mayonnaise
50 g/2 oz cheese
salt and pepper
12 large, thin slices bread

Makes 24

Put the eggs in a small saucepan and pour in enough cold water to cover them. Put the pan on the hob and turn the heat to high. As soon as the water boils, turn the heat down to medium. Boil the eggs for 10 minutes. Turn the heat off. Pour off most of the boiling water down the sink. Run cold water over the eggs in the pan, then leave them to cool.

Crack the eggs and peel off the shells. Put them in a basin and mash them with a fork until they are very fine. Stir in the mayonnaise. Grate the cheese and mix it into the eggs with some salt and pepper.

Cut the crusts off the bread. Spread a slice with some of the egg mixture. Roll it up from the short side, pressing it firmly together without squeezing out the filling. If the bread will not stay rolled, put 2 cocktail sticks through it. Cut the roll in half.

Make all the other rolls, then pack them close together in a container or in cling film. The cocktail sticks may be removed when the sandwiches are packed.

Pizza sticks

100 g/4 oz plain flour
50 g/2 oz margarine
½ teaspoon dried marjoram
50 g/2 oz cheese
salt and pepper
1 teaspoon tomato purée
1 tablespoon water
extra plain flour
beaten egg or milk, to glaze

Makes 12

Set the oven at 200°C/400°F/gas 6. Grease a baking tray. Sprinkle a little flour on the work surface, then gently knead the dough until smooth. Flatten it into a big sausage, then cut this into 12 equal pieces. Roll the pieces of dough into thin sticks measuring about 15cm/6 in long. *1*

Put the dough sticks on the greased baking tray, leaving a little room between them. Brush them with a little beaten egg or milk. Bake for 15–20 minutes, until the sticks are golden brown. *2*

While the sticks are baking, set out a wire rack to put them on. Put a heatproof mat on the work surface. Turn off the heat. Use oven gloves to take the baking tray from the oven. Use a palette knife or slice to lift the pizza sticks off the tray and put them on the wire rack to cool. *3*

Put the flour in a bowl. Add the margarine, then use a knife to cut the margarine into small pieces. Rub the fat into the flour. *4*

Add the marjoram. Grate the cheese on the coarse side of the grater and add it to the mixture. Stir in some salt and pepper. In a mug or small basin, mix the tomato purée with the water, then add the mixture to the dry ingredients. Use a palette knife or a blunt knife to mix the ingredients together. When the mixture forms large lumps, use your fingers to press it together into a ball. *5*

▪▸· *mini flans* ·◂▪

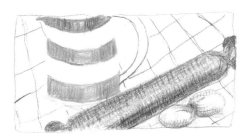

1   Set the oven at 190°C/375°F/gas 5. Have ready 15 patty tins. Put the flour in a bowl. Add the margarine and cut it into small pieces. Use your fingers to rub the margarine into the flour. The mixture is ready when it looks like fine breadcrumbs.

2   Add the cold water to the pastry, then use a blunt knife to mix it together. If the pastry does not form clumps add just a few more drops of water. Press the pastry into a ball.

3   Sprinkle a little flour on the work surface and on your rolling pin. Roll out the pastry thinly. Use a 6–7.5 cm/2½–3 in cutter to cut out 15 circles of pastry. Dip the cutter in flour so it does not stick to the pastry. Put a circle of pastry in each patty tin, pressing it in neatly.

4   Make the filling. Put the soft cheese in a bowl. Trim the bad bits off the spring onions, wash and dry them. Cut them across into small pieces, then mix them with the cheese.

5   Stir in the eggs. Grate the cheese and add it to the filling with a little salt and pepper. Stir well. Use a teaspoon to put this filling into the tartlets.

6   Bake the tartlets for 20–25 minutes. They should be brown and set on top. Have a heatproof mat or board ready to put the tray on. Use oven gloves to lift the tin. Turn off the oven. Leave the flans in the tins for 10 minutes. Have ready a wire rack. Then use a palette knife to help lift them from the tins and put them on a wire rack to cool.

*225 g/8 oz plain flour
100 g/4 oz margarine
about 2 tablespoons cold water*

Filling
*225 g/8 oz soft cheese (cream or curd cheese)
4 spring onions
2 eggs
50 g/2 oz cheese
salt and pepper*

Makes 15

▎►·*vegetable* **d***ippers* ·◄▎

These are easy to make. Use some or all of the following vegetables.

celery sticks
carrots
cauliflower florets
radishes
cucumbers
red or green peppers
spring onions

1 Scrub celery sticks under cold running water. Trim the ends, then cut the sticks into 5 cm/2 in lengths.

2 Peel carrots and cut off their ends. Cut them in half lengthways. Cut each piece in half lengthways, then across to make neat sticks.

3 Cut the thick stalk off a cauliflower. Separate the head into small florets. Wash and dry them.

4 Trim the tops of radishes and wash them. Dry on absorbent kitchen paper.

5 Peel cucumber and cut it into 5 cm/2 in lengths. Stand each piece up and cut down into quarters.

6 Cut peppers in half. Cut out the stalk, core and seeds. Cut the peppers across into 1 cm/½ in wide pieces.

7 Trim any bad bits off spring onions. Cut off the green part (save it for a salad or put it in the dip), leaving 5 cm/2 in of the white part.

▎►·*cottage* **c***heese* **d***ip* ·◄▎

225 g/8 oz cottage cheese
4 tablespoons mayonnaise
4 tablespoons snipped chives
1 tablespoon tomato purée
salt and pepper

Serves 6

1 Put a sieve over a bowl. Turn the cottage cheese into the sieve. Use a wooden spoon to rub all the cheese through the sieve. Scrape the cheese off the underneath of the sieve when you have finished.

2 Add the mayonnaise, chives and tomato purée. Mix well, then sprinkle in a little salt and pepper. Stir to mix in the seasoning. Cover with cling film and chill the dip for 30 minutes.

SNIPPED CHIVES

3 Chives are long, thin and green – they look a bit like grass. They taste like onions. They should be washed, then dried on absorbent kitchen paper and snipped. All this is much easier if you hold the bunch of chives together neatly. Holding the bunch firmly at one end, use a pair of scissors to snip the chives into tiny bits. Gradually move your fingers back so you can cut up the whole bunch.

COOKIE HUNT

This is a good idea for an indoor or out-door party. Simply invite your friends to come over for a cookie hunt.

We are having a cookie hunt on
Wednesday April 6th
at 75 Holly Close
Please come at 4 pm.
Love
Sarah

Cut out circles of paper to look like cookies and write your invitations on them. If you like, draw a circle in the middle to look like icing and add a cherry. Or, draw light brown cookies with dark dots for chocolate chips.

WHAT TO PLAN

★ Make lots of different cookies.
★ Wrap the cookies in cling film then wrap them in coloured paper.
★ Just before the party, hide the cookies all over the house. In summer you can have a cookie hunt in the garden.
★ Give prizes for the child who finds the most cookies.
★ Have a prize for the child who finds the largest cookie.
★ Have a prize for the child who finds the best decorated cookie.
★ Have a booby prize for anyone who does not find a single cookie.

COOKIE HATS

If you like, ask everyone to come wearing a cookie hat. These can be made from cardboard and tied on with string. They should have different decorations on top. Some hats could look like sandwich cookies, others like chocolate chip cookies or iced cookies. Give a prize for the best cookie hat.

Cookie Hunt Menu
Pizza Sticks (page 65)
Vegetable Dippers (page 67)
Cottage Cheese Dip (page 67)
Lots of different cookies
Chocolate Milk Shakes

▸· basic biscuits ·◂

225 g/8 oz plain flour
½ teaspoon baking powder
100 g/4 oz butter or margarine
40 g/1½ oz icing sugar
2 egg yolks
1 teaspoon vanilla essence

Makes 30–35

1

2

3

4

5

6

Set the oven at 180°C/350°F/gas 4. Grease 2 baking trays. Put the flour and baking powder in a bowl. Add the butter or margarine and cut it into small pieces. Use your fingertips to rub the fat into the flour. The mixture is ready when it looks like breadcrumbs.

Stir in the icing sugar. Make a well in the middle of the mixture. Put in the egg yolk and vanilla essence. Stir the egg and vanilla into the rubbed in mixture until it forms clumps. Then use your fingers to press the mixture together into a dough.

Cut the dough in half. Put a little flour on the work surface and on your rolling pin. Knead 1 piece of dough into a smooth flat round, then roll it out to about 5 mm/¼ in thick. Use cutters to cut out the biscuits.

Cut the biscuits in all sorts of different shapes. Re-roll all the trimmings. Repeat with the second portion of dough.

Put the biscuits on the baking trays. Bake for about 15 minutes, until lightly browned.

Use oven gloves to take the trays from the oven. Turn off the heat. Use a palette knife to lift the biscuits off the trays. Put them on the wire rack to cool. Add toppings and decorations to the cold biscuits.

TOPPINGS

★ Melted chocolate with chopped nuts.
★ Glacé icing. Follow the instructions for making the icing used on Clever Cookies (page 15). Top the biscuits with halved cherries or chocolate polka dots.
★ Melt 2 tablespoons crunchy peanut butter with 100 g/4 oz chocolate.
★ Orange icing – mix 100 g/4 oz icing sugar with 1–2 tablespoons orange juice.

DECORATIONS

★ Coloured sugar strands or chocolate strands
★ Chocolate buttons, milk and white
★ Small jellied sweets
★ Silver balls
★ Mimosa balls
★ Halved or quartered glacé cherries with strips of angelica
★ Flaked almonds

DIFFERENT FLAVOURED BISCUITS

Chocolate – add 2 tablespoons cocoa powder with the icing sugar.
St Clement's – add the grated rind of 1 lemon and 1 orange with the icing sugar.
Walnut – add 50 g/2 oz finely chopped walnuts with the icing sugar.
Chocolate Chip – stick chocolate polka dots into the cookies before baking them.

▸·peanut cookies·◂

75 g/3 oz soft margarine
75 g/3 oz soft light brown sugar
1 teaspoon vanilla essence
100 g/4 oz self-raising flour
75 g/3 oz salted peanuts

Makes about 15

1 Set the oven at 180°C/350°F/gas 4. Grease 2 baking trays. Put the margarine in a bowl with the sugar. Beat well until the mixture is very soft and light.

2 Stir in the vanilla essence. Add all the flour and the peanuts. Mix well until all the ingredients are combined. The mixture will make a soft dough.

3 Take small lumps of the dough and roll them into balls about the size of walnuts. Place the balls well apart on the baking trays. Flatten the balls with a fork. Bake for about 15 minutes, until golden.

4 Put out a wire rack. Use oven gloves to remove the trays from the oven. Have a heatproof mat ready. Turn off the heat. Leave the cookies on the trays for 2 minutes, then use a palette knife to put them on the wire rack. Leave until cold.

▸· pinwheel biscuits ·◂

1 quantity Basic Biscuits (page 69)
2 tablespoons cocoa powder

Makes about 32

1 Set the oven at 180°C/350°F/gas 4. Grease 2 baking trays. Make up the biscuit dough. Cut it in half. Put a little flour on the work surface. Knead 1 piece of dough into a smooth flat round. Put 1 tablespoon cocoa in the middle. Fold the dough around the cocoa. Knead the dough until all the cocoa is mixed in. Mix in the rest of the cocoa in the same way.

2 Lightly flour the work surface and the rolling pin. Roll out the chocolate dough to an oblong measuring 25 × 20 cm/10 × 8 in. Set this aside. Knead the plain dough into a smooth flat round, then roll out to the same size.

3 Put the rolling pin on the chocolate dough and roll the dough over it. Lift the dough on top of the plain dough. Lightly press the two layers of dough together.

4 Roll up the dough from the long end like a Swiss roll. Press it together firmly. Use a sharp knife to cut the roll into 32 5 mm/¼ in slices. Put these on the baking trays. Bake for 15–20 minutes.

5 Use oven gloves to take the pinwheels from the oven. Have a heatproof mat ready. Use a palette knife to lift the pinwheels from the trays. Put them on the rack to cool.

▸· chocolate milk shakes ·◂

2 tablespoons cocoa powder
3 tablespoons boiling water
about 1 tablespoon sugar
600 ml/1 pint cold milk
4 chocolate Flakes

Makes 4

1 Put the cocoa in a large heatproof jug. Carefully mix in the boiling water. Stir in the sugar. Whisking all the time, slowly pour in the milk. Whisk until the milk is frothy.

2 Pour the shakes into 4 small glasses and put a chocolate Flake in each.

ROLLER PARTY

Invite your mates to a roller disco, then take them home for something to eat. If you prefer you could organize a skate-boarding party, a swimming party, a trip to the theatre or to the cinema. Take advantage of whatever is going on in the area.

WHAT TO PLAN

★ Where to go – check out facilities at youth centres and sports centres. Ask for details of reduced prices for parties. See what is on at the theatre or cinema.

Make sure your parents are involved in your plans.
★ Invite everyone to meet at your house before going on to the entertainment. Your parents should plan the transport.

PARTY PLANNING

★ Have a bright paper tablecloth with matching paper napkins
★ Have plastic or paper plates
★ Decorate the room with streamers and balloons
★ If you want to play music, choose the records

Menu
Nutty Eggs
(page 22)
Sesame Cheese
Puffs (page 28)
Stuffed
Tomatoes
Savoury Rolls
Coleslaw Cups
(page 27)
Garlic Bread
Lemon Jelly
Cheesecake

▶ Savoury rolls ◀

*1 onion
25 g/1 oz butter or margarine
100 g/4 oz fresh breadcrumbs
100 g/4 oz chopped mix nuts
3 tablespoons chopped parsley
1 teaspoon dried mixed herbs
50 g/2 oz cheese
1 egg
225 g/8 oz puff pastry dough (thawed if frozen)
beaten egg, to glaze*

Makes 18

1 Set the oven at 220°C/425°F/gas 7. Grease 2 baking trays. Peel and chop the onion. Put the butter or margarine in a small saucepan. Put the pan on the hob and turn the heat to medium. When the fat has melted add the onion. Cook, stirring occasionally, for 5 minutes. Turn off the heat.

2 Put the breadcrumbs, onion, nuts, parsley and dried herbs in a bowl. Add the grated cheese to the mixture. Add the egg with a little salt and pepper. Mix well to combine all the ingredients.

3 Sprinkle a little flour on the work surface and on your rolling pin. Roll out the pastry dough into an oblong measuring 30 × 45 cm/12 × 18 in. Cut this in half lengthwise. Divide the breadcrumb mixture in half. Use a teaspoon to put half all down the middle of 1 strip of pastry. Put the rest down the second strip of pastry. Brush the edges of the pastry with a little water and fold them over to completely cover the filling.

4 Press the pastry edges together firmly. Cut the rolls into 5 cm/2 in lengths. Press the filling in at the ends. Put the rolls on the baking trays with the join in the pastry underneath. Brush a beaten egg over the top. Bake for 10–15 minutes, until the pastry is puffed and golden. Set out a wire rack and heatproof mat. Use oven gloves to put the rolls on the rack to cool.

▪►·$tuffed tomatoes·◄▪

*2 eggs
6 medium tomatoes
50 g/2 oz fresh breadcrumbs
2 tablespoons snipped chives
2 tablespoons chopped parsley
parsley sprigs, to garnish*

Makes 6

Boil your eggs (see Nutty Eggs on page 22) and shell them when they are cool. Put them in a small basin and mash well.

Cut a thin slice off the top and chop into small pieces. Scoop out the soft middle, putting it all in a basin.

Drain the tomatoes upside down on kitchen paper. Add the breadcrumbs, chives and parsley to the basin.

Mix well, sprinkling in some salt and pepper.

Mix in the mashed egg with the tomato and breadcrumb mixture.

Use a teaspoon. Arrange the stuffed tomatoes on a plate. Garnish with parsley sprigs.

·►·garlic bread·◄·

50 g/2 oz butter
1 small clove garlic
1 tablespoon chopped parsley
1 short French loaf

Makes 10 pieces

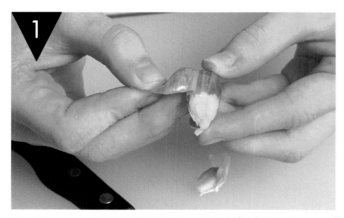

Set the oven at 200°C/400°F/gas 6. Put the butter in a small basin and soften it by creaming it with the back of a wooden spoon. Peel the garlic and put the clove in a garlic crusher.

Crush the garlic into the butter, scraping all the bits off the crusher. Add the parsley and mix well.

Cut the loaf into 10 slices. Lay a piece of foil, large enough to wrap the loaf, on the work surface. Spread the butter thinly on the slices and press them all back together on the piece of foil. Fold the foil around the loaf, pinching the edges together to seal the packet.

Put the bread in the oven for 10–15 minutes, until all the butter has melted and the bread is hot and crisp. Have a basket ready and put some absorbent kitchen paper or a napkin in it. Use oven gloves to remove the bread from the oven. Turn the heat off. Open the foil very carefully as steam will come out. Put the bread in the basket and serve at once.

·lemon jelly cheesecake·

Put the biscuits in a polythene bag. Twist the end of the bag closed but do not seal it. Use a rolling pin to crush the biscuits in the bag. Do this fairly gently so as not to break the bag.

1

Put the butter in a medium saucepan. Put the pan on the hob and turn the heat to medium. When the butter has melted, turn the heat off. Add the biscuits to the butter and stir. Turn the biscuits into a 23 cm/9 in flan dish. Scrape all the bits from the saucepan. Press the biscuits evenly over the base of the dish. Put the dish in the refrigerator.

2

Break the jelly into squares and put them in a basin. Pour the boiling water over the jelly. Stir until the cubes have dissolved completely. Leave until cold, then put the jelly in the refrigerator until it is just beginning to set. It should be rather like syrup.

3

Put the cheese in a bowl. Add a little jelly and beat well. Gradually beat in all the jelly. Turn this mixture into the flan dish. Spread it evenly over the biscuit base. Put the cheesecake in the refrigerator until it is set.

4

Turn the cream into a basin and use a whisk to whip it until it is thick enough to stand up in soft peaks. Put a star piping nozzle in a piping bag. Put the nozzle and the bag in a measuring jug, folding the ends of the bag over the outside of the jug. Spoon the cream into the bag, scraping every little bit out of the basin.

5

Gather up the ends of the piping bag and twist them together. Hold the nozzle near the edge of the cheese-cake and squeeze out some cream. At the same time gently move the bag round to pipe a swirl. Pipe swirls all around the edge of the cheesecake. Put chocolate buttons between the swirls. Cut the cheesecake into wedges to serve.

6

100 g/4 oz plain sweet biscuits
50 g/2 oz butter
1 lemon jelly tablet
300 ml/½ pint boiling water
500 g/1 lb cream cheese
150 ml/¼ pint double cream
chocolate buttons, to decorate

Serves 12

TEATIME TREAT

Making a special tea for the rest of the family, or for 1 or 2 friends, can be fun. Make a special cake and some sandwiches. Turn bought ice cream into a real treat with peach slices. To make the table look special add a posy of flowers and tie pretty ribbon bows around some paper napkins.

TABLE POSY

Find a small vase or a small pot. Cut small flowers to make a table decoration. If you want to tie a bow of ribbon around the pot it is best to do this first. If you use narrow ribbon you can tie several small bows and leave the ends of the ribbon to trail prettily. Pour some water into the pot, then add the flower.

DECORATIVE NAPKINS

Wrap a piece of ribbon loosely around each paper napkin, then tie it in a bow. If you like, put a small flower in the bow just before tea.

LAYING THE TABLE

Put a tablecloth on the table and put your flowers in the centre. Put out a knife and plate for each person. Arrange the napkins on the plates. Set cups and saucers (if you need them) separately on a tray so the tea can be poured easily.

Teatime Menu
Sandwich Rolls (page 65)
One-stage Carrot Cake
Peach Melba
Iced Tea

▶ *One-stage Carrot Cake* ◀

175 g/6 oz grated carrots
100 g/4 oz soft margarine
100 g/4 oz caster sugar
175 g/6 oz self-raising flour
1 teaspoon baking powder
1 teaspoon ground cinnamon
2 eggs
50 g/2 oz raisins
100 g/4 oz walnut pieces
1 orange

Cream Cheese Frosting
225 g/8 oz cream cheese
2 tablespoons icing sugar
2 tablespoons orange juice
a few walnut halves, to decorate

Makes an 18 cm/7 in cake

DECORATION IDEA
You can make some marzipan carrots to decorate the cake. Make them the day before you are going to decorate the cake. Colour about 100 g/4 oz marzipan with a little orange food colouring. Knead the colour into the marzipan until it is evenly mixed. Cut the marzipan into 6 pieces. Roll each piece into a short sausage, then shape them into carrots, with a point at one end and a thick part at the other end. Pat the thick end of the marzipan flat. Stick a few thin pieces of angelica into the flat end of each carrot. Very gently mark lines across the carrots.

1 Take a piece of greaseproof paper and stand an 18 cm/ 7 in deep round cake tin on it. Draw around the bottom of the tin. Cut out the circle of paper. Grease the tin and put the paper in the bottom of it. Grease the paper. Set the oven at 160°C/325°F/gas 3.

2 It is important to grate the carrots before you weigh them. Cut off their ends and peel them, then grate the carrots on the medium-fine side of the grater. Eat any chunks left over at the end of grating! Put the weighed carrots in a bowl.

3 Add the margarine, sugar, flour, baking powder and cinnamon. Break 1 egg into a cup, then tip it into the bowl. Break the second egg and tip it in. Add the raisins and walnuts. Now mix all the ingredients together until they are thoroughly combined. The mixture should be soft and creamy.

4 Grate the rind off the orange. Stir it into the cake mixture, then turn the mixture into the tin. Use a plastic spatula to scrape all the mixture from the bowl. Spread the mixture evenly in the tin. Bake the cake for 1½ hours.

5 The cake is cooked when it is risen and golden brown. To test if the middle is cooked, stick a clean, metal skewer into the cake. Take the skewer out again. If there is any sticky mixture on the skewer the cake is not cooked in the middle.

6 Set out a wire rack. Use oven gloves to lift the cake from the oven. Turn it out on to the rack to cool.

7 To make the Cream Cheese Frosting, put the soft cheese in a bowl. Add the icing sugar and orange juice. Beat well until the cheese is soft and smooth.

8 Put a doily on a plate and put the cake on it. Spread the frosting thickly on top of the cake. Use a knife to make large swirls in the frosting. Decorate the cake with walnut halves. Tie a large bow of ribbon around the side of the cake.

▸ peach melba ◂

*225 g/8 oz raspberries
4 tablespoons icing sugar
425 g/15 oz can peach slices
8 scoops bought vanilla ice cream*

Serves 4

1 Place a sieve over a bowl. Put the raspberries in the sieve and use a spoon to press them through. Scrape the raspberry purée from underneath the sieve when you have finished.

2 Stir the icing sugar into the raspberry purée.

3 Open the can of peaches and drain off the liquid. Divide the peach slices between 4 glass bowls. When you are ready to serve the Peach Melbas, put 2 scoops of ice cream into each bowl. Spoon the raspberry sauce over the tops. Serve at once.

▸ iced tea ◂

*2 Earl Grey tea bags
900 ml/1½ pints boiling water
4 lemon slices
4 sprigs of mint
4 ice cubes*

Serves 4

1 Put the tea bags in a heatproof jug or in a teapot. The water must be freshly boiling in the kettle. Pour it into a measuring jug, then pour it straight on to the tea bags. Take great care when using the kettle and pouring boiling water. Ask an adult to stand near by.

2 Leave the tea for 7 minutes. Use a spoon to lift out the tea bags. If the tea is in a pot there is no need to lift out the bags but the tea should be poured into a heatproof jug. Cover the jug with cling film and leave the tea until cold. Put the tea in the refrigerator for at least 30 minutes.

3 Pour the tea into 4 glasses. Add an ice cube to each. Float a slice of lemon on the tea and add a sprig of mint to each glass. Offer a bowl of caster sugar with the tea.

THE BRUNCH BUNCH

Be a trend-setter and invite your friends to a brunch party. Plan to go out after you have eaten your brunch or organize party games and stay at home. Brunch is ideal if you want to go out to the cinema afterwards or if you want to go for a walk.

Brunch combines both breakfast and lunch at about 11.30 am. Remember to put the time on the invitation and let your friends know what you have planned for afterwards.

*Tim invites you to brunch
on Saturday 6th June
at 44 Georgie Villas.
Afterwards we shall be going to see the new
Space Thrill movie at the cinema.
Please come at 11.30 am.
Love
Tim*

WHAT TO PLAN

★ If you want to go to the cinema or to any other form of entertainment make sure you allow enough time for eating and for getting there.
★ Make sure that walks or transport are organized by the adults.
★ If you are planning a walk, make sure all your guests come with suitable clothes and shoes.

Brunch Menu
Grapefruit Cocktails
Bacon Kebabs with Granary bread rolls
Banana Muffins (page 33)
Yogurt Fizz

▶· yogurt fizz ·◀

600 ml 1/1 pint natural yogurt
fizzy orange drink
4 orange slices

Serves 4

1 Spoon the yogurt into 4 glasses. Add a little fizzy orange and stir. Top up with more fizzy orange.

2 Cut a slit into the centre of each orange slice. Slip the slices over the rim of the glasses and put drinking straws into each Yogurt Fizz. Serve at once.

▶· grapefruit cocktails ·◀

2 large grapefruit
2 large oranges
about 4 teaspoons clear honey
4 mint sprigs

Makes 4

1 Cut a slice off each fruit. Stand a grapefruit on a board and cut strips of peel down the side until all the peel and pith are removed. Repeat with all the fruit.

2 When the fruit is peeled, cut it into slices. Pick out the pips and cut the slices into chunks. Put these in a basin and mix well. Cover and chill for at least 1 hour.

3 Divide the fruit between 4 small glass bowls and trickle about 1 teaspoon of honey over each. Top with a mint sprig. Stand the glass bowls on saucers. Put a teaspoon on each saucer.

▶· bacon kebabs ·◀

4 rashers rindless bacon
4 skinless sausages
4 small tomatoes
8 button mushrooms
a little vegetable oil
4 Granary rolls
a little butter or margarine
watercress sprigs, to garnish

Serves 4

Cut the bacon rashers in half. Roll up each piece. Cut the sausages in half. Cut the tomatoes in half.

Trim off the ends of the mushrooms stalks. Rinse the mushrooms, wiping off any dirt, and dry them on absorbent kitchen paper.

Thread all the prepared ingredients on to 4 skewers. Turn the grill on high. Brush a little oil over the kebabs and cook them under the grill for 5–8 minutes, until the sausages and bacon are browned on one side. Turn the kebabs over and cook the other side. Meanwhile, split and butter the Granary rolls.

Have 4 plates ready. Turn the heat off and put 1 kebab on each plate. Garnish with watercress sprigs. Put a split and buttered Granary roll on each plate and serve at once.

SUMMER GARDEN PARTY

Invite friends to a summer garden party or plan a little treat for the rest of the family. On really hot summer days people always used to wear hats to keep the sun off their heads. So, make your garden party a hat party. Tell your friends or the family they have to wear a hat.

THE BEST HATS

Have a prize for the best hat. Silly hats are easy to make. They can be made from coloured paper with all sorts of bits and pieces glued on. Or a plain, old hat may be used as the base for a clever design. Add lots of flowers, bows or even artificial fruit to create a stunning hat!

THE HAT RACE

You will need 2 hats with ties sewn on. Divide the party into 2 teams. Each team has a hat. The teams stand in a line and the person at the front holds the hat. At the signal to 'go' the first person puts the hat on and ties it under their chin. Then he or she unties it and takes it off, quickly passing it to the next person. Everyone has to put the hat on, tie and untie it before passing it on. When the hat gets to the last person they tie the hat on and rush to the front. The first team to finish is the winner. Don't forget to have little prizes for the winners.

WHAT'S IN THE HAT?

This is a game for the family. Have a deep hat and put 6–10 things in it. Give every person a blindfold – a scarf to tie around their eyes will do. The hat full of things is passed around and every person has to decide what it contains by feeling the different objects. Each person is only allowed 1 minute to feel the bits and pieces. Ask everyone in turn if they can remember what was in the hat. The winner is the one who gets the most right. Find clever things to put in the hat: a torch, a pin cushion (without pins) and so on.

WHAT TO PLAN

★ If you have just a few friends you may be able to sit around a table. If not have rugs out so you can sit on the lawn.
★ Plan some outdoor games – try some of the ideas for the Picnic Party (page 63). Pack and hide little gifts in the garden, then let your friends find them.
★ Remember to make a hat to wear.
★ Have 1 or 2 spare hats just in case someone forgets to bring their own.

Garden Party Menu
Ham Triangles
Stuffed Cucumber
Celery Boats
Strawberry Tartlets
Fruit Punch

ham triangles

50 g/2 oz butter or margarine
8 thin slices bread
a little mustard
8 slices cooked ham
mustard and cress, to garnish

Makes 16

1. Place the butter in a basin and soften with a spoon. Cut the crusts off the bread and spread with butter.

2. Spread 4 slices with a little mustard. Place a slice of ham on top, then put the remaining bread on top, buttered sides down, to make sandwiches.

3. Cut the sandwiches across into 4 triangles. Arrange these on a plate and cover with cling film until you are ready to serve them. Put a few small bunches of mustard and cress around the sandwiches for garnish.

Stuffed Cucumber

20 cm/8 in piece cucumber
50 g/2 oz soft cheese with garlic and herbs
50 g/2 oz cooked ham or boneless chicken
8 parsley sprigs

Makes 8 pieces

1. Peel the cucumber. Cut it into 8 slices measuring 2.5 cm/1 in thick. Use a teaspoon to scrape the middle out of the cucumbers. Do this carefully, taking out just the soft part with the seeds. Put a double thick piece of absorbent kitchen paper on a plate and put the pieces of cucumber, cut sides down, on it to dry.

2. Put the soft cheese in a basin. Cut the ham or chicken into thin strips. Cut the strips across into very small dice. Add the ham to the cheese and mix well.

3. Put a little of the cheese into each piece of cucumber. Use a teaspoon and a knife to push it into the hole in the middle of the cucumber. Place the stuffed cucumber on a plate and put a sprig of parsley on top.

Strawberry tartlets

1 quantity pastry as for Mini Flans (page 66)
2 tablespoons icing sugar
1 teaspoon vanilla essence
500 g/1 lb strawberries
100 g/4 oz strawberry jam
1 tablespoon water

Makes 15

Set the oven at 200°C/400°F/gas 6. Prepare all the ingredients for the pastry and make it following the recipe. Add the icing sugar to the dry mixture when you have rubbed the fat into the flour. Add the vanilla essence with the water. Line 15 patty tins following the recipe.

Prick the pastry cases 2 or 3 times with a fork. Bake them for 10–15 minutes, until they are lightly browned. Set out a heatproof mat. Use oven gloves to take the tins from the oven and then put it on the mat. Turn the heat off.

Leave the pastry cases in the tins for 5 minutes, then carefully lift them out using a palette knife. Put them on a wire rack to cool.

Wash and dry the strawberries. Twist the stalks and pull out the thin cores.

Put the jam in a basin with the water. Put some water into a small saucepan and put it on the hob. Put the basin on the saucepan and turn the heat to medium. Stir the jam until it has melted. Turn off the heat. Leave the basin over the hot water.

Fill the tartlet cases with strawberries. Cut some of the strawberries in half if they are very big. Use oven gloves to take the basin of jam off the water. Brush the melted jam all over the strawberries in the tartlets. Leave to set before serving.

▸·celery boats·◂

3 celery sticks
100 g / 4 oz high fat soft cheese
a little paprika

Makes about 15

Trim the ends of the celery. Scrub the celery under cold water to remove all the dirt. Drain and dry the sticks on absorbent kitchen paper.

Cut the celery into 5 cm/2 in lengths. Put the cheese in a basin and mix it with a spoon until it is soft.

Put a star nozzle into a piping bag. Put the nozzle and the piping bag into a measuring jug, folding the ends of the bag over the outside of the jug. Spoon the cheese into the bag.

Gather up the ends of the piping bag and twist them together to enclose the cream cheese. Twist the ends of the bag together until the cream cheese is right down in the nozzle. Hold the nozzle over a piece of celery. Hold the celery with one hand and squeeze some cream cheese on to it in a neat line.

Pipe cream cheese on to all the celery pieces. Sprinkle just a little paprika on the tops. Arrange the Celery Boats on a plate. If you like put the celery and cucumber on the same plate.

▸·fruity punch·◂

1 orange
1 lemon
2 tablespoons blackcurrant syrup
150 ml / ¼ pint apple juice
1 large bottle sparkling mineral water

Makes 8 glasses

Prepare the orange and lemon the day before. Cut both into thin slices. Cover a small baking tray with cling film and lay the slices on it. Put them in a freezer until they are hard.

Mix the blackcurrant syrup and apple juice in a jug. Pour in the mineral water. Add the frozen fruit slices. Leave for 5–10 minutes before serving. The frozen fruit slices cool the drink instead of ice cubes.

FINGER-LICKIN' LUNCH

Make lunch for the family or for your friends. This is a buffet lunch, so you can serve lots of bought snacks like crisps.

TABLE DECORATIONS

The type of decorations will depend on the time of year.

Spring – Have a yellow paper tablecloth, yellow napkins and bowls of fresh green and yellow ribbons. You can have posies of miniature daffodils on the table. Easter Monday is a good day to make a lunch treat. Put tiny baskets of miniature chocolate eggs on the table.

Summer – In summer put small posies of flowers and huge bows on each corner of the table. Choose pink and pale green ribbons, and tie pretty bows with long ends. Use a pink or white paper tablecloth. Have pink and green paper napkins and arrange them in fans on the plates.

Autumn – Make small posies of dried flowers. If you have a Hallowe'en lunch, put a hollowed out pumpkin with a face cut in it on the table. Stand a small night light in the pumpkin. Have rust, dark green and brown paper napkins and bows of ribbons in the same colours.

Winter – Decorate a winter table with bright red ribbon and fir cones. Add some fresh green ivy. Use bright red and green napkins with small bows of matching ribbons. For Christmas, add lots of holly, small baubles and tinsel. If you have candle holders, put candles on the table – they brighten up a dark winter day.

WHAT TO PLAN

Plan a simple indoor game that everyone will enjoy. For example, try charades. Everyone writes the name of a book, film, object, or animal on a piece of paper. The papers are folded and put in a bag. Everyone picks out a piece of paper. In turn they mime whatever is written on their piece of paper. The others have to guess what was written on the paper.

Finger-lickin' Lunch Menu
Tuna Fish Dip
Cottage Cheese Dip (page 67)
Vegetable Dippers (page 67)
Crisps and nuts
Pâté Toasts
Spicy Sausage Bites
Open Rolls
Easy Trifle
Homemade Lemonade

►· Open rolls ·◄

4 finger rolls
50 g/2 oz butter or margarine
4 cheese slices
24 slices cucumber

Makes 8

Split the rolls in half. Put the butter in a basin and soften it with a spoon. Spread the butter or margarine on the rolls.

Cut the cheese slices in half. Cut each half into 3 pieces. Put 3 pieces of cheese and 3 slices of cucumber on each roll, overlapping them alternately.

Arrange the rolls on a plate and cover with cling film until ready to serve.

►· tuna fish dip ·◄

200 g/7 oz can tuna
100 g/4 oz soft cheese with herbs and garlic
6 tablespoons mayonnaise or natural yogurt
salt and pepper

Serves 6

Open the can of tuna and drain off the liquid. Put the tuna in a basin and mash it with a form until it is all broken into small shreds.

Add the soft cheese and mix well. Stir in the mayonnaise with salt and pepper to taste.

Put the dip in a dish. Cover with cling film and put it in the refrigerator until you are ready to put the food on the table.

►· pâté toasts ·◄

100 g/4 oz smooth pâté
12 Melba toasts
3–4 radishes
12 parsley sprigs

Makes 12

If the pâté is firm, put it in a basin and soften it by beating with a wooden spoon. Carefully spread the pâté on the Melba toasts. Do this flat on a board. The Melba toasts will break if you try to spread the pâté on them on a plate.

Cut the radishes into thin slices. Arrange some slices of radish and a sprig of parsley on each piece of toast. Put the Pâté Toasts on a plate and cover with cling film until ready to serve.

▸· spicy sausage bites ·◂

*8 skinless sausages
1 teaspoon curry powder
1 clove garlic
1 tablespoon tomato ketchup
1 tablespoon natural yogurt or lemon juice
salt and pepper
1 tablespoon vegetable oil
1 small jar cocktail onions
1 grapefruit (optional)*

Makes 32

1 Cut the sausages into 4 pieces. Put the curry powder in a large basin. Crush the garlic in a garlic crusher over the basin. Scrape all the bits from the outside of the crusher.

2 Add the tomato ketchup, yogurt or lemon juice to the curry powder. Sprinkle in a little salt and pepper. Put the pieces of sausage in the basin and mix well with a spoon. Carry on mixing up the sausages until all the pieces are flavoured with the curry paste.

3 Put a frying pan on the hob. Add the oil and turn the heat to medium. After 1 minute the oil will be hot and it will run freely over the pan if you tilt it. Add all the sausages. Cook for 15–20 minutes, stirring the sausages often so they brown all over.

4 Put a double thick piece of absorbent kitchen paper in a bowl. Turn the heat off. Tip all the sausages on to the paper. Shake the paper a little, then leave the sausages to cool.

5 Drain the onions. Thread each piece of sausage on to a cocktail stick with an onion. Put all the bites on a plate or stick them into a grapefruit.

▸· homemade lemonade ·◂

*2 large lemons
175 g/6 oz sugar
4 tablespoons water
1 large bottle sparkling mineral water
ice cubes
lemon slices, to serve (optional)*

Makes 8 glasses

1 Grate the rind off both lemons on a fine grater. Put the rind in a saucepan. Cut the lemons in half and squeeze out all their juice. Add this to the pan.

2 Add the sugar and water to the pan. Put the pan on the hob and turn the heat to medium. Cook, stirring until the sugar has dissolved completely. Turn the heat off. Leave the lemon syrup to cool.

3 Put the cold syrup in a jug, topped up with mineral water. Add ice cubes and lemon slices if you like.

▶· easy cherry trifle ·◀

1 large Swiss roll
3 tablespoons orange juice
425 g/15 oz can cherry pie filling
425 g/15 oz can custard
150 ml/¼ pint double cream
25 g/1 oz flaked almonds
6–8 maraschino or glacé cherries
6–8 small strips angelica

Serves 4–6

Cut the Swiss roll into thin slices. Put them in the bottom of a glass dish and about a third of the way up the side. Put any extra slices in a second layer on the bottom of the dish. Sprinkle the orange juice over the Swiss roll. Open the can of pie filling and use a spoon to spread it evenly over the Swiss roll.

Open the can of custard and pour it into a bowl, scraping all the custard out of the can. Put the cream in a basin and use a whisk to whip it until it stands in soft peaks. Add all the cream to the custard. Use a spatula to scrape the basin. Use a large metal spoon to fold the cream into the custard. Spread this all over the cherry pie filling.

Put the trifle in the refrigerator for at least 1 hour, better still, leave it overnight. Heat the grill to high. Put a piece of foil on the grill rack and sprinkle the almonds on it. Brown the almonds under grill. Watch them all the time as they burn very easily. Use a long-handled wooden spoon to turn them once or twice. Turn the grill off and leave the almonds to cool.

Sprinkle the almonds over the trifle. Stick a small piece of angelica into each cherry. Arrange the cherries around the trifle just before serving it.

A GIFT FROM THE COOK

▸· special dates and walnuts ·◂

6 dates
12 walnut halves
75 g/3 oz soft cheese with herbs and garlic

Makes 12

1 Use a small pointed knife to make a cut down the length of each date. Carefully pick out the stones from the middle of the dates.

2 Take a small teaspoon and put a little of the soft cheese into each date. Take care not to make a mess on the outside of the dates. Spread the remaining cheese on the flat side of 6 of the walnuts. Press the other 6 walnut halves on to the cheese.

3 Put the dates and walnuts in paper sweet cases and pack them in a small box. Cover with cling film and store in the refrigerator.

▸· stilton bites ·◂

50 g/2 oz Stilton cheese
50 g/2 oz butter
75 g/3 oz plain flour
12 blanched almonds

Makes 12

1 Put the cheese in a basin and mash it with a fork until it is reduced to small crumbs. Add the butter use a wooden spoon to mix it with the cheese. Beat the mixture until it is soft. Tip the flour into the basin and stir it into the cheese mixture to make a soft dough. Use a knife to mark the dough in half, then into quarters.

2 Grease a baking tray. From each quarter of the dough you should roll 3 balls. Put the balls on the baking tray, well apart. Flatten each ball slightly and press a blanched almond on top. Put the baking tray in the refrigerator for 30 minutes to chill the cheese balls.

3 Set the oven at 200°C/400°F/gas 6. Bake the cheese balls for 15–20 minutes, until they are golden. Have a heatproof mat ready. Set out a wire rack. Use oven gloves to take the baking tray from the oven. Use a palette knife to lift the Stilton Bites off the tray and put them on the wire rack to cool. Turn the oven off.

4 When they are cold, pack the Stilton Bites in a box. Line the container with a paper napkin and cover with cling film.

peanut Crunch

225g/8 oz sugar
150 ml/¼ pint water
100 g/4 oz salted peanuts
25 g/1 oz butter
¼ teaspoon bicarbonate of soda

Makes an 18 cm/7 in square

1 Put the sugar in a saucepan. Pour in the water. Put the pan on the hob. Now prepare all the other ingredients before cooking.

2 Have the peanuts near the hob ready to add to the caramel. Put the butter on a small saucer near the hob. Put the bicarbonate of soda in its measuring spoon on a saucer near the hob. Lastly, grease an 18 cm/7 in square tin. Stand the tin on a wooden board.

3 Turn the heat to medium and stir the sugar and water until the sugar has dissolved completely. Do not stir the syrup again. Turn the heat to high and bring the syrup to the boil. Turn the heat down slightly but keep the syrup boiling and bubbling rapidly.

4 Watch the syrup all the time but do not stir it. After a while it will begin to change colour, turning very pale brown. Once it begins to turn brown it will brown quickly.

5 When it is a light golden colour (like syrup) turn the heat off. Add all the peanuts, butter and bicarbonate of soda. Stir quickly to mix the nuts into the caramel. The bicarbonate of soda will make it frothy.

6 Use oven gloves to lift the pan from the hob. Pour the mixture into the greased tin. Scrape it all out of the pan. Put the pan in the sink and fill it with water otherwise it will be difficult to wash.

7 Leave the mixture until it is completely cold and hard. Break it into chunks with the handle of a wooden spoon. Pack the chunks in a polythene bag and put an airtight clip on them.

HELP POINT
Boiling sugar syrup is tricky and it can be dangerous. Always make sure you have an adult with you.

hazelnut truffles

175g/6 oz chocolate
50 g/2 oz unsalted butter
50 g/2 oz toasted chopped skinned hazelnuts
1 tablespoon orange juice
1 tablespoon single cream or fromage frais
or Greek-style yogurt
cocoa powder for coating

Makes about 20

Simple coffee cake truffles

100g/4 oz chocolate
175 g/6 oz plain cake
2 teaspoons instant coffee
2 tablespoons boiling water
chocolate vermicelli for coating

Makes about 20

Hazelnut truffles

1. Break the chocolate into pieces and put them in a heatproof basin. Add the butter. Pour some water into a small saucepan and put it on the hob. Turn the heat to medium.

2. Stand the basin over the saucepan of water. Stir the chocolate and butter until both are completely melted. Do not allow the water to boil up at all. Turn the heat to low if the water begins to boil.

3. Turn the heat off and use oven gloves to lift the basin off the saucepan. Stir in the hazelnuts and orange juice. Leave the mixture to cool for about 30 minutes.

4. Stir the cream, fromage frais or yogurt into the chocolate, then put the basin in the refrigerator until the chocolate is firm enough to shape into balls. This will take about 45 minutes. It can be left for longer, then allowed to stand at room temperature for a while to soften slightly.

5. Put a small pile of cocoa on a plate. Set out about 20 paper sweet cases. Wash your hands under cold water and dry them. Try to keep your hands cold while you roll the truffles to stop you getting into a sticky mess!

6. Take a teaspoonful of the mixture and drop it on the cocoa. Roll it quickly into a ball and put it in a paper sweet case. Shape all the remaining truffles then put them in the refrigerator for at least 1 hour before packing them in a box. Cover with cling film. Add a bow and a tag.

Simple coffee cake truffles

1. Break the chocolate into squares and put them in a heatproof basin. Pour some water into a small saucepan and put it on the hob. Turn the heat to medium. Stand the basin over the saucepan. Stir the chocolate until it melts. Turn the heat to low if the water begins to boil.

2. Turn the heat off and use oven gloves to lift the basin off the saucepan.

3. Put the cake in a bowl. Wash and dry your hands. Crumble the cake with your fingertips until it is all in tiny crumbs.

4. Put the coffee in a cup and add the boiling water. Stir well. Use a teaspoon to sprinkle this coffee all over the cake. Pour the melted chocolate over the cake. Scrape all the chocolate out of the basin.

5. Use a spoon to mix the cake with the chocolate and coffee. Stir it for some time until it is all really well mixed up.

6. Put a small pile of chocolate vermicelli on a plate. Set out about 20 paper sweet cases on a baking tray. Wash and dry your hands again.

7. Take small spoonfuls of the mixture and shape it into balls. Roll the balls in the vermicelli, then put them into paper cases. Put the truffles in the refrigerator for at least 1 hour before you pack them in a box and cover with cling film. Add a bow and a tag.

·◄· quick peppermint creams ·◄·

*a little icing sugar
225 g/8 oz packet fondant icing (icing to roll out)
peppermint essence
green food colouring*

Makes about 30

HELP POINT
*Take care not to add too much green
colouring. Just add a drop at a time or the
colour will be too dark.*

1 Set out a small baking tray. Lay a sheet of cling film on it and sprinkle icing sugar over the film.

2 Place just a little icing sugar on the work surface. Unwrap the icing and knead it lightly into a smooth ball. Dip a cocktail stick into the peppermint essence and dab it on to the icing. Knead it again. Do this until all the icing is flavoured with peppermint. Taste a tiny pinch of icing. Add more essence if needed.

3 Cut the piece of icing in half. Wrap one half in cling film and set aside. Cut the other piece into about 15 equal lumps. Roll each lump into a smooth ball, then flatten it into a smooth round.

4 Dip your fingertip in a little icing sugar. Rub the side and top of the sweet very gently with your fingertip to make it smooth and shiny. Place on the baking tray. Roll and flatten the other white sweets.

5 Unwrap the other piece of icing. Dip a cocktail stick into the green food colouring and drop just a little on to the icing. Knead it until it is all evenly pale green. Shape into sweets as for the white icing.

6 Leave the peppermint creams to dry for 2–3 hours. Put them into paper sweet cases, then place them in a box and cover with cling film. Add a bow and a tag.

chocolate fruits

These are fun to make and they taste really good. You may use different sorts of fruit. Here are some fruits you may like to try:

*green grapes on their stalks
strawberries with stalks
cherries with stalks
segments of mandarin orange*

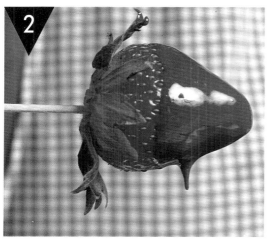

1 Use dark plain chocolate, milk chocolate or white chocolate. It is best to melt too much chocolate so it is easy to dip the fruit. Leave any leftover chocolate in the basin until it hardens, then take it out, wrap it in cling film and keep it in the refrigerator until next time.

2 Gently wash the fruit and dry it on absorbent kitchen paper. Lay a sheet of non-stick baking paper on a baking tray and put it near the hob.

3 Have all the fruit for dipping on a large plate. Break some chocolate (at least 225 g/8 oz) into squares and place them in a heatproof basin.

4 Put some water into a saucepan and put it on the hob. Stand the basin over the saucepan and turn the heat to medium. Stir the chocolate until it has dissolved completely. Lower the heat if the water begins to boil.

5 Use oven gloves to lift the basin off the pan. Pick up a piece of fruit and dip it into the chocolate so it is half covered. Lift it out and let the excess chocolate drip back into the basin. Give the fruit a gentle twist and put it on the paper-lined tray.

6 When all the fruit is dipped leave the chocolate to set completely before placing them in paper sweet cases. If you prefer put the fruits in a small dish without the paper cases. Cover with cling film.

·►· *marzipan fruits* ·◄·

225g/8 oz marzipan (white marzipan is best)
red, green, yellow and orange food colourings
a few cloves

Makes about 24

1 Wash and dry your hands. Put a sheet of cling film on a baking tray. Get all the food colours and a very fine paint brush ready.

2 Knead the marzipan until it is soft. Break off a small piece and roll it into a ball. Mould the ball into a thin sausage shape to look like a banana. Curve it slightly and flatten it along one side. Make a very tiny stalk shape at one end. Put the banana on the baking tray.

3 To shape a strawberry, roll out a piece of marzipan into a ball, then mould a pointed end and flatten the opposite end. Make a very small, flat circle of marzipan and cut it all round the edge into points to look like strawberry leaves. Brush a tiny drop of water on the leaves and stick it on the flat end of the fruit.

4 Shaping oranges is easy. Just roll out some marzipan into a ball and flatten the top slightly. Make an apple in the same way, moulding it with a slightly flatter top.

5 When you are moulding the fruit put the same types near each other on the tray. Paint them with food colouring. Paint just 1 colour at a time.

6 Paint the bananas yellow, the strawberries red, the strawberry leaves and the apples green and the orange with orange. Wash and dry the brush before starting a new colour.

7 Now add the features to the fruit. Use a very tiny grater (one used for grating nutmeg) to mark the skin on the oranges. Use a cocktail stick to mark the dents in the strawberries. Mark small creases around the top of the apple using a cocktail stick.

8 When the colours are dry, use brown colouring to paint fine lines on the banana and paint the stalk. Leave the fruits overnight.

9 Put the fruits in paper sweet cases and pack them in a box. Cover with cling film.

⊪►·*Sweet popcorn*·◄⊪

2 tablespoons vegetable oil
2 tablespoons popping corn
2 tablespoons sugar

Makes 1 bag

POPCORN SPECIALS
★ *Popcorn is good savoury as well as sweet. Do not add the sugar. Instead, add a knob of butter and 2 table-spoons of grated Parmesan cheese to the corn and stir for about 1 min-ute. Sprinkle with a little salt and paprika, then leave to cool.*
★ *Instead of sugar, trickle 2 table-spoons honey over the popcorn and stir for a few seconds until the corn is golden. Turn into the basin to cool.*
★ *Mix the cold corn with raisins and nuts to make a bag of mixed nibbles.*

1 You will need a fairly large saucepan which has a lid. Have a heatproof basin ready to hold the cooked pop-corn. Pour the oil into the pan and put it on the hob. Heat the oil over medium heat for about 2 minutes.

2 Add all the corn to the pan and put the lid on. Turn the heat to high until the corn begins to pop. When the corn is popping turn the heat to the lowest setting. Shake the pan occasionally and cook the corn until the popping has stopped.

3 Use oven gloves to lift the lid off the pan. Sprinkle the sugar over the popcorn and stir well. Turn the heat to a high setting and stir the corn until the sugar melts and browns. This should take less than a minute. Take care not to overcook the popcorn or the sugar will burn.

4 When the corn is lightly browned and beginning to stick together, turn it all into the basin and leave it until it is cold. Do not taste the popcorn until it is cold as the caramelized sugar is very hot.

5 Pour cold water into the saucepan to soak otherwise the sugar hardens on it. Pack the cold popcorn in a polythene bag and seal it with a metal tie. Tie ribbon and a tag on the bag.

·►· *toffee apples* ·◄·

4 red apples
4 wooden skewers
225 g / 8 oz sugar
150 ml / ¼ pint water

Makes 4

Wash and thoroughly dry the apples, then polish them with absorbent kitchen paper until they shine. Place a piece of non-stick cooking paper on a baking tray. Stick a wooden skewer into the core of each apple and stand them on the baking tray.

Put the sugar in a saucepan. Pour in the water. Put the pan on the hob. Turn the heat to medium and stir the sugar and water until the sugar has dissolved completely. Do not stir the syrup again. Turn the heat to high and bring the syrup to the boil. Turn the heat down slightly but keep the syrup boiling and bubbling rapidly.

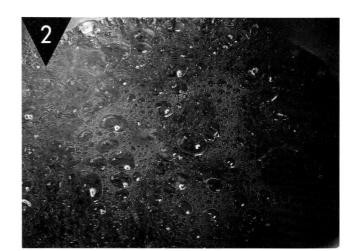

Watch the syrup all the time but do not stir it. After a while it will begin to change colour, turning very pale brown. Once it begins to turn brown it will brown quickly.

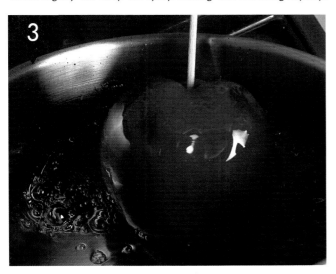

When it is slight golden colour (like syrup) turn the heat off. Hold the apples by their sticks and dip them quickly in the caramel. Tilt the pan slightly if necessary to coat the apples and twist them around.

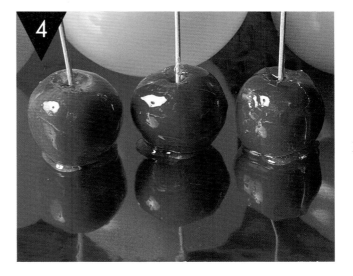

Let the excess caramel drip off back into the basin, then twist each apple to catch the last of the drips and put it back on the tray. Leave until the caramel is cold and hard. Do not keep the apples longer than 2 days or they become very sticky.

INDEX